Also by John Antrobus for BearManor Media

THE MILLIGAN PAPERS
Six BBC Radio comedy scripts
(The last series Spike Milligan did for the BBC)

INVITATION TO A PLAGUE
A murder has occurred in an incurable ward. All the patients will die within a few weeks so it makes an investigation pretty meaningless, as Inspector Hedge points out to his Superintendent. However, he might discover a germ warfare experiment has leaked into the community...

THE HORSE MUTINY
The stories of three horses in World War One

GOON BUT NOT FORGOTTEN

John Antrobus

GOON BUT NOT FORGOTTEN

© 2021 John Antrobus. All Rights Reserved.

No portion of this publication may be reproduced, stored, and/or copied electronically (except for academic use as a source), nor transmitted in any form or by any means without the prior written permission of the publisher and/or author.

Published in the USA by
BearManor Media
1317 Edgewater Dr. #110
Orlando, FL 32804
www.BearManorMedia.com

Paperback edition
ISBN: 978-1-62933-706-7
Hardcover edition
ISBN: 978-1-62933-707-4

INTRODUCTION

This book is a journey up river deep into the jungle-like *Apocalypse Now* minds of Peter Sellers and Spike Milligan? Put them in a hall of mirrors and they would look fine, for they were distorted before they stepped in and the twisted mirrors would straighten them out. They were competitors in madness, it was the breath of their publicity, the calculation of their fortune. Sellers made it to Hollywood, Milligan to Cricklewood – or nearby to the BBC at Shepherds Bush. Were there moments of sanity? Undoubtably, unavoidably, even days and weeks but these were periods of respite before onward up-river! Harry Secombe, the fine and funny third Arch-Goon, escapes my attention. He went on from Goon Show days to TV shows that I was not involved in and onward to sing in his fine Welsh voice on *Songs Of Praise* on television. Thus he was saved and I am happy for him.

This started as a book of sketches I wrote for the Goons and a couple of short stories added, half reminiscence, half hallucination. There you go, what you perceive as reality is just that... what you perceive! My publisher asks me to comment on why I wrote this book? Why anything? Do I need to excuse myself for being so generally unemployable that I will write anything, or draw, or sing or dance, or act, rather than take a job? And doing the most unlikely thing is more likely to be the most rewarding. Please try it...

The world admired and loved the Goons for what they presented, an endless show, but hush hush sweet Charlotte at three in the morning it was only God that could save them with a sweet silence from their endless charades. The brightest light casts the darkest shadow. Not that I have dwelt on this aspect. Nor that when I eventually returned down-river from that heart of darkness known as comedy writing my hair had turned white – and so it remained.

In writing this book, I have enlisted Sherlock Holmes and Watson to help me track down these two genies that escaped their bottle – that smashed their bottles never to return. It proved to be a dangerous work of detection as will be revealed. A case that could have changed for ever their very roles so loved by us...

Up-river. Pulled into jetty and found abandoned stockade. Weird sound of laughter from a hut. Inside was a guy, calm, methodical, but what lay under the surface I could only guess.

Was that you laughing?

Yes, forgive me. Thanks for telling me that was the sound of me laughing. I wondered what it was? I am the editor of the Goon Show Preservation Society quarterly magazine (GSPS).

Would you be interested in editing my book?

Of course. The Arch Goons in spirit are further up-river. The memorabilia stops here. I would not recommend anyone to venture further, you might not return.

That's how I met Peter Embling. I did return and much thanks to Peter for editing this book.

Sitting in a Saigon bar, dimly lit, in fact lit only by the light of my imagination I ask myself will anything ever be more than a reflection of myself? If not then do I like what I'm seeing? Can I witness the miracle?

Life is.

In the doing is the life energy and that is the turn on! So come – take your partner – populate your own dance floor! It is the earth under your feet...

Big thanks to Ben Ohmart my publisher, off the wall enough to be an Honorary Goon.

Shall we dance?

*'When you're blue and lowdown don't get into a trance
Just jump into a dustbin and dance, dance, DANCE!'*

The Mad March Days of 2021. 'Dare Mighty Things...'

John Antrobus

GOON BUT NOT FORGOTTEN

I squeezed past a crate of vegetables that tottered and asked me to dance. Declining the invitation, I climbed the narrow stairs on mildewed carpet that led above the green grocers shop – on the wall I noticed a framed cheque for one million pounds with the instructions,

> IN CASE OF BANKRUPTCY BREAK GLASS AND
> CASH CHEQUE IMMEDIATELY.

I arrived in the reception area of Associated London Scripts. They are waiting for you upstairs said the ever-cheerful Pam Vertue, sister of Beryl Vertue, with such a nice smile and was further directed upstairs. The aroma of vegetables fading I entered Spike's office. Peter Sellers beamed at me.

Peter: Hello, young John. Where have you come from?
Spike: He's come from downstairs.
Peter: Downstairs? There is so much of it! It spreads out into the street and Heaven knows where?
Spike: I know. It's terrifying.
Peter: Try not to think of it. John? That's an unusual name. John? Why could it not have been Fluganaghan? What took you so long to get here, John?
Me: I was born in Woolwich. But lost my way.
Spike: He went to the Royal Military Academy, Sandhurst. John Antrobus was an officer cadet.
Peter: Really? What did they train him to do?
Spike: They trained him to leave the army.
Me: I became a pacifist.
Peter: Ah, that's a principle worth fighting for! I was going to be a pacifist but I didn't fancy jumping out of an aeroplane…

Everybody laughed or we were laughing already and we repaired to Bertorelli's across Shepherd's Bush Green for lunch.

Let me show you to a table gentlemen, greeted the effusive maître d'.
I have not come here to buy furniture! My good man, exclaimed Sellers. I have three of your tables at home already. We require food. Nourishment!
In that case, sir, let me give you our menus – in Braille.
We are not blind, you fool! said Milligan
You will be if you attempt to drink the house wine, said the maître d'.
If you are going to joke like that, I hope you are a fully paid up member of Equity, replied Sellers.
I am indeed, smirked the maître d'. I would like a spot on your radio show.
The only spot you will get is a spot on my bottom, said Sellers. Bring us a bottle of champagne immediately and direct us to Portsmouth where we will launch a battleship.
I was at a restaurant once and the waiter serving us had a heart attack and died at our table. I said.
What did you do? asked Sellers.
Well, I complained to the maître d' and ordered a fresh waiter.
I got a laugh. I was in.
Can you write that up as a sketch for me? asked Sellers.
Yes, of course…
He's not available, said Spike. He's working for me.
Are you going to pay him money? enquired Sellers.
Yes. To cure his poverty, said Milligan. But not too much, it would drive him mad. John is not used to money. I showed him a five pound note in my office and he fainted from the sight of it.
The poor boy, said Sellers. Were you clothed at the time?
No, I was naked. I had just come back from the bank. I had an appointment with the manager.
Of course, muttered Peter. They are all filthy swine. A manager at Coutts once insisted on taking me down to the vaults and showing me my overdraft. It was quite dark down there and it was in a terrible state…
It needed money, interjected Spike. Your poor thin overdraft, Peter.
It was thin, of course, said Peter. Very thin but the money was not going to come from me! I let the fellow know, this bank manager chappie. They've got plenty of money, haven't they? They were not going to get mine as well. I changed my account to Bradley and Bingley's that very morning and then I went home and changed out of my bathing suit and put my snorkelling equipment away.
Yes, said Spike. They are so formal at these banks. Mine has a changing room.

To change currency?
No, to change your underwear, Peter.
Good idea. Peter said to me, John! You of youthful talent vigour and naivety – after lunch would you like to come with me and visit a medium?
That's where he goes to get his steaks, said Spike. Medium rare.
Harry Secombe, the third of the Goons, breezed in, Hello! Hello! Hello! Hello folks! And all who support you in your nefarious endeavours!
Am I late?
What for? asked Peter.
For being rude and insulting to everyone?
No, not at all. We have managed very well to be insulting without you.
I am disappointed. Harry collapsed at the table in a pool of Secombe. I was held up in the traffic so I lowered the car window and sang Abide With Me. He sang, Fast falls the eventide!
And did it fall fast? demanded Spike.
No, it's still daylight! You can't win them all can you? Have you already eaten?
Yes, daily since I was born, declared Sellers. It helped me to grow to this incredible size. I started as a baby. I cannot imagine how it happened.
It is a miracle, said Harry. I will order a haircut and chop suey.
This is not a Chinese restaurant or a hairdressers Harry, said Spike. It is Italian and they have surrendered.
I don't see any white flags!
The tablecloths are white, you fool!
Then we've won! Shouted Secombe. This calls for a celebration! More wine! Flowers! Dancing girls!! We'll soon be on the boat home, lads! And demobilised! I can marry the girl of my dreams and dream of the girl I didn't marry!
Later, after a merry repast, Peter changed his mind.
Forget the medium today. I'll phone him to cancel.
Can't you do it by thought transference, Peter? asked Spike. It would be cheaper.
There is nothing cheap about me, Spike. How dare you insinuate that I am on the verge of bankruptcy! Which of course I am! You swine! Have at your wallet!
I was at the doctors this morning, replied Spike. And he operated on my wallet and removed thirty pounds.
Just in time, said Peter. A swollen wallet is a desperate condition bringing hallucinations of future prosperity. When more likely there will have to be a

whip round to pay for your funeral. Meanwhile who is paying for lunch today? I am temporarily embarrassed which is very embarrassing...

* * * * *

IDIOT WEEKLY PRICE TUPPENCE

Peter Sellers and the then up and coming talented director, Dick (Richard) Lester had the idea that Goon humour would work on television. No, said Spike Milligan, it is a verbal medium – that's where it works – so count me out. Spike would change his mind soon enough but he was absent from the early recordings. I was one of the principal writers roped in to contribute to Idiot Weekly...

> A poor young Marks and Spencer's trainee manager lay dying
> Out on the lone prairie
> His thin legs so bare
> Lay with him there
> And they sang in harmony
> Take my false teeth back to Ireland
> And give them to Mother Macree
> For a Marks and Spencer's trainee manager's last wish is
> Oh please wash the dishes
> That drove you away from me...

Sang the Goon-sheet covered Peter Sellers to the accompaniment of the mock-Edwardian Alberts. We were recording one of the first television programmes for Associated Rediffusion. The following sketch became Peter Sellers' favourite that he loved to play with Graham Stark:

"KITCHENER SKETCH"

STREET. LARGE KITCHENER POSTER ON WALL "KITCHENER NEEDS YOU".
DOORWAY BESIDE IT. MATE AS STREET CLEANER COMES PAST, USING BRUSH.
HE SEES POSTER. PUTS ON FALSE BEARD, DUCKS UNDER POSTER AND THE FINGER OF KITCHENER WHICH IS POINTING AT HIM.
AS MATE COMES UP THE OTHER SIDE OF POSTER (TAKING OFF

FALSE BEARD), THE RECRUITING SERGEANT (SELLERS) STEPS OUT OF THE DOORWAY.

SERGEANT:
Hello, hello…
MATE:
Hello.
SERGEANT:
Hello, hello – and what have we here – and how are you today?
MATE:
Very well.
SERGEANT:
Very well – oh, that's very good, that is. Oh yes, oh yes.
MATE:
Is it?
SERGEANT:
Oh, yes – yes, yes – have you seen 'im?
MATE:
'im?
SERGEANT:
Points at poster… 'im.
MATE:
Oh, 'im.
SERGEANT:
Yes, 'im. He Needs You…
MATE:
Does 'e?
SERGEANT:
Oh, yes – oh, yes, yes … 'e needs <u>you</u> over <u>there…</u>
MATE:
Oh.
SERGEANT:
Oh, yes – yes … 'e sent me back 'ere from over there – 'e did. Oh, yes… Do you know what 'e said before I left?
MATE:
No, I don't, mate.
SERGEANT:
'e said go back over there…
MATE:
Over there…

SERGEANT:
Over 'ere… 'e said – and get _'im_.
MATE:
Points at poster… _'im_.
SERGEANT:
Points at mate… _'im_.
MATE:
Me?
SERGEANT:
You…
MATE:
Oh.
SERGEANT:
Oh, yes – oh, yes – get _'im_, 'e said, and bring 'em back over _'ere_.
MATE:
'ere.
SERGEANT:
Over _there_ – over _there_… cos _'e_'s all ready, you know – oh, yes…
MATE:
Is 'e?
SERGEANT:
Oh, yes – to launch the big attack – against _them_.
MATE:
Them?
SERGEANT:
Them… But 'e won't launch it…
MATE:
Won't 'e?
SERGEANT:
Not without _you_.
MATE:
Points at Sergeant. You…
SERGEANT:
Points at Mate. You…
MATE:
Me?
SERGEANT:
Oh, yes… So you'd better hurry, 'adn't you…
Sergeant shoves rifle – bayonet fixed – into Mate's arms.

So's <u>you</u> can join '<u>im</u> over <u>there</u> from '<u>ere</u> and <u>us</u>.
MATE:
Us…
SERGEANT:
Can launch the attack against <u>them.</u>
MATE:
Them – us – 'ere…
SERGEANT:
<u>There</u> – over <u>there</u>… There's Germany!
Points off. Now CHAAARGE!!!

MATE RUNS OFF WITH RIFLE AND BAYONET, FEEBLY YELLING.

* * * * *

When was it the following happened? Is there a time line? Memory makes of time what it will providing deep fissures in a landscape of recollections into which we may plunge into guilt remorse regret…

I was with Spike Milligan – that I know – in his office and we were writing. It was early days when he was still with his first wife June and his children were his magical kingdom. Spike had a shelf of box files and then another shelf. It is obvious that his mania to control a domestic situation was unravelling as he tried to control expenses. The box files, the documents of expenditure, the income tax the income tax the Inland Revenue so many boxes each a weight and Harrods that was a file all on its own. He pulled it off the shelf and exclaimed,

June is going to Harrods today, shopping. I begged her not to. No I didn't beg. I will not beg. Does she think she can control me? Punish me by a spending spree to match my ability to provide for my family? What motivates her? Is it to punish me? See what she has spent at Harrods alone this financial year it would wreck a lesser household that is why I spend so much time here at my office writing writing, John, sometimes with you but into the night ideas maybe I can sell…

He passed his hand to his forehead and rubbed it. And continued, June would drive me into a mental hospital – it has happened before – I had been sleeping at the office to pay the bills but she said I was neglecting the family not being at home. He nodded, well this time she will not break me. She wanted me to have lunch with her today at Harrods. I said no I cannot I cannot I must write I cannot afford the time for such a lunch break today and please do not spend too much June! Do not spend! We have everything! Everything we need! You are not dressed in rags June why do you keep saying so, your wardrobe is full! Pairs of shoes everywhere I said! Some hardly worn once maybe! Don't buy more shoes I said and left for work, John, I am a simple artisan. My needs are simple. I am a worker. A socialist. At times I am and friends with Michael Foot. Ah well…

Spike sighed and returned the Harrods box file to the shelf. We resumed our writing session, it was going well when the phone rang. It was reception, Janet downstairs who asked him would he take the call? Yes, he said and listened silently until he said I will come immediately I will be there shortly. He put the phone down with an air of resignation. That was the Harrods manager he explained. June has had a breakdown in one of their departments. She was trying on a pair of shoes and burst into tears. I must go to her. I'll probably take her to lunch afterwards. Sorry John. You see she has won again. Stay as long as you like, John, come up with a few ideas. I don't know when I'll be back. If ever…

Spike grabbed the car keys from the desk.

Will you buy her the new shoes? I asked.

Of course, he said. I will not lose face in front of a Harrods floor manager. And I'll probably buy an electric lawn mower. He hurried out of the office.

I stayed a while but nothing came so I went home walking through the park a pleasant afternoon. I was to marry soon. Would that be destined to become another wreck in the comedy hahaha landscape?

* * * * *

Peter Sellers would often recall sketches I wrote for him including the *"ART GALLERY"* sketch. This he first performed, again with his chum Graham Stark, on *IDIOT WEEKLY*. Later also on the *JO STAFFORD SHOW* for ITV:

SETTING: AN ART GALLERY

ENTER JULES (GRAHAM), and JIM (PETER).

JIM:
Jules! Jules! Oh look.
JULES:
What have you found, Jim?

JIM:
A Van Gogh. The Cornfields. Oh it is beautiful.
JULES:
Truly remarkable.
JIM:
Perfect.
JULES:
Harmony sublime.
JIM:
Van Gogh is my favourite painter. He says it all, Jules.
JULES:
He does indeed, Jim. He is the master.
JIM:
Yes. And this picture must be his greatest. It was his best period. Provence.
JULES:
Yes. His madness transpires humanity.
JIM:
True, yes.
JULES:
Yes, yes, yes.
JIM:
(Pause) Although you know somehow I think it would be a little more balanced if he placed a haystack there...
(He takes out a crayon and draws a haystack on the painting.)
If Vincent had done this...
JULES:
I'm sure he would have been grateful for that.
JIM:
Do you think so?
JULES:
Yes, Jim, I do.
(Takes out crayon and draws on painting)
Although to balance that – to harmonise, I feel a cottage up here would be perfectly placed.
JIM:
Oh, yes, perfect. But this would mean colouring the field here to add texture.
(He scribbles away)
JULES:
I agree – if I add a little fox here – for atmosphere.

JIM:
Yes. And a family that picnic, here – by the stream.
JULES:
What stream?
JIM:
I am drawing it.
(They draw feverishly)
JULES:
I will help you. It comes from this mountain lake.
JIM:
What mountains?
JULES:
These mountains.
JIM:
Oh yes.
JULES:
Yes, yes, yes!

THEY STAND BACK AND ADMIRE THEIR WORK.

JIM:
There is no doubt about it.
JULES:
True.
JIM:
Van Gogh is a great artist.
JULES:
The best. The very best. A genius. I worship before him.
JIM: (Looks away).
Jules. Look. A Rodin?

JIM TAKES OUT A CHISEL AND MALLET. HE MOVES AWAY.

JULES:
Rodin! I love Rodin! Wait for me, Jim! Yes, I agree. He doesn't need that extra arm! Superb!

JULES TOO MOVES OUT OF THE PICTURE. MOVE INTO CU OF DEFACED VAN GOGH.
SFX OFF: CHISEL AND MALLET BREAKING MARBLE.

*****

One day out of rehearsal Peter said, Come and meet my mother. We drove to Muswell Hill where as it happened my mother was brought up.

My Grandad worked on the Metropolitan Water Board round here, I said. But he sprang a leak so he was retired early. During the First World War he was an air raid warden looking out for German Zeppelin bombers.

Did he find any, John?

I don't know. They didn't tell him where to look so he was searching women's handbags.

Hang on, said Peter. There's someone I know.

He pulled the car up to the curb and hailed a gentleman. Hello, Alf! John, this is Alf Slynne, my estate agent. Alf, this is John Antrobus.

The gentleman said, John Antrobus? I nearly married your mother! I could have been your father! It was a close shave I must say!

Peter creased up, as he kept repeating in genteel cockney after we had moved on, I could have been your father! I nearly married your mother! It was a close shave I must say!

Yes, I said. He used to watch my mother shave her legs. Or maybe he didn't.

Where was your father then?

He was posted to India for three years. In the army. He was a jealous man, my Dad. Possessive. He couldn't bear anybody else sharing what he loved. That's why he shot his dog before he came back to England.

Of course, said Peter. Lucky he didn't shoot your mother before he went to India.

We fell about laughing.

Sitting in the kitchen having tea I found Sellers' mother to be a charming lady, an ex-music-hall performer. Peter speaks very highly of you, she said.

Seven foot six, said Peter.

That's much higher than other people believe me. Sometimes he has a very low opinion of people.

Spike Milligan, two foot six.

I thought you'd made up with Spike?

Oh yes. He's normal height today. For an Irishman lying down.

Can't you be serious for a moment, Peter? He's either like this or he's suicidal.

Yes, I drove to Beachy Head last weekend but there was such a queue to jump off I came home.

Did you put your name down? I asked.

Yes, on a scrap of paper. They put it in a bottle and threw it off the cliff.

That will have to do for now, said his Mum. How are Ann and the children?

I was going to ask you that, said Peter.

Why? Haven't you been home recently?

Yes, Mum. I had breakfast there this morning.

So how was your wife?

I don't know. She didn't tell me. I don't do domestic, Mum. I'm very busy at the moment recording a TV show.

You've still got a family, Peter.

Thanks for reminding me. I do know my duties. I'm the bread winner, OK? No argument there. And the cake winner. And the icing on the cake.

He does very well, said Peg. But my son works too hard. Show business isn't all fun. I should know. Our Peter was born in a trunk.

Yes, I had to find a locksmith to get out. Not easy when you're ten years old.

He could have done a Houdini act, my son! He's so talented! But Peter chose comedy.

To alleviate the suffering, Mum. It was either that or take up smoking which would be bad for my health.

We were all laughing at the badinage. I could see that Peter had a strong bond with his mother.

I'm sorry you've got to go now, she said.

We've only just arrived, Mum.

I'm still sorry you've got to go, she said.

Why? He demanded.

Because, son, I find it so saddening every time we part – we never know when it's the last time, do we? So I'd rather get it over with if you don't mind. Mind you, when I do go, Peter – when I cross over – I shall be in touch from the world of the spirits. And I'll keep a place for you in Heaven, son.

I don't want to be sitting next to angels, he said. Because I'm allergic to feathers, you know that, Mum.

I know you are with ducks, she said.

Well angels aren't that different, are they? I mean they're all flying around, aren't they? Mum, it doesn't matter. Anyway there's no hurry to go is there? To cross over?

You never know, do you? she said. Well, as you're here you might as well have another cup of tea. Where's the tea-strainer?

It's his day off, said Peter.

* * * * *

Here's another *IDIOT WEEKLY* sketch, performed by Peter Sellers and Graham Stark.

"POLICE SKETCH" Idiot Weekly. (Associated Rediffusion, 1958)

SUPERINTENDENT'S OFFICE AT SCOTLAND YARD. THE SUPERINTENDENT IS SITTING BEHIND HIS DESK. A BARBER IS BUSILY CUTTING HIS HAIR.
A CONSTABLE COMES IN.

CONSTABLE:
There's a gentleman to see you, sir.
SUPERINTENDENT:
Send him in.

THE BARBER HAS FINISHED HIS HAIR AND TAKES THE APRON FROM ROUND THE SUPERINTENDENT'S NECK. HOLDS THE MIRROR UP.

SUPERINTENDENT:
Splendid. He takes a purse out. How much do I owe you?
BARBER:
Well, sir, let's say whatever you'd like to give.

THE SUPERINTENDENT PUTS THE PURSE BACK IN HIS POCKET.

SUPERINTENDENT:
Very reasonable. Next Thursday then, same time. Good day to you.

BARBER EXITS AND TWITT COMES IN WITH CONSTABLE.

CONSTABLE:
The gentleman, sir.
(He exits.)
TWITT:
Tentatively.
My name is Twitt, Superintendent. Mr Twitt.
SUPERINTENDENT:
Not without good reason, I'm sure. Edge towards my desk.

TWITT:
Edge?

TWITT TRIES TO MAKE HIMSELF AS INCONSPICUOUS AS POSSIBLE AS HE CROSSES THE ROOM TO THE DESK.

TWITT:
I would like to have a private chat with you, Superintendent.
SUPERINTENDENT:
Well, why won't you pop in and see me sometime?
TWITT:
I have… now…
Sits.
SUPERINTENDENT:
So you have. What luck – or as they say in French – quel luck. You will excuse me if I finish this letter while we chat, won't you? It's rather important.
TWITT:
Well, it's like this, Superintendent. I've been getting threatening letters – regularly.
SUPERINTENDENT:
Yes, the Post Office are very good with their deliveries, aren't they? How do you spell strangle, Mr Twitt?
TWITT:
STR… AN… GLE…
SUPERINTENDENT:
Thank you…
TWITT:
Every morning when I come down to breakfast one of these terrible letters is lying there – on the doormat.
SUPERINTENDENT:
On the doormat, you say?
TWITT:
Yes.
SUPERINTENDENT:
At least we know where they are coming from then. Is there an 'i' in disfigure?
TWITT:
I think there is… I just don't understand. I mean, what pleasure can it give

anyone writing these awful things?

CLOSE-UP OF SUPERINTENDENT

SUPERINTENDENT:
Engrossed in letter… And kick your cat… dig up your garden… burn your house… and hit you… and smash you… twist your neck into gut… and… I'm sorry, what were you saying?
TWITT:
What pleasure can it give anyone to write such horrible things?
SUPERINTENDENT:
I don't know, my dear chap. We can only guess what goes on inside a mind like that.

THEY STARE AT EACH OTHER.

TWITT:
Yes.
SUPERINTENDENT:
Yes… Now, where's an envelope? Here we are… writes. Three Plunger Crescent, The Grove…
TWITT:
But that's my address. That's where I live.
SUPERINTENDENT:
Is it really? Perhaps you wouldn't mind popping this in for me then, as long as it's on the doormat breakfast time tomorrow.
TWITT:
Oh yes, that will be a great pleasure, that will. Wait a minute. The handwriting on this envelope is the same as the writing on the threatening letters…
SUPERINTENDENT:
Let me see…
Takes letter.
By Jove, you're right. I think we're onto something. Check for fingerprints. Could I have your finger.

TAKES TWITT'S FINGERPRINTS.

SUPERINTENDENT:
A perfect tally. Your fingerprints are on this letter. They stand up. And it hasn't even been delivered to you yet… And you just gave it to me, didn't you?

TWITT protests.

SUPERINTENDENT:
Look, the ink's not even dry. You've got a lot to explain. Constable!

CONSTABLE ENTERS.

SUPERINTENDENT
To constable. Take this man to the cells.

CONSTABLE EXITS WITH TWITT.
CLOSE-UP OF SUPERINTENDENT AT DESK.

SUPERINTENDENT
Another case solved… I hope you enjoyed that insight into the workings of the Force. Now, if you'll excuse me, I have some very important letters to attend to…
Dear Vicar, last night I saw your wife in the park with the gardener. Your daughter also was…

FADE

* * * * *

We were driving back to the centre of town and Peter asked me, How was Alf Slynne nearly your father?

I don't know, I said. My Dad only met my Mum for six weeks before he went to India. They got engaged before he left. He was in the Royal Artillery on embrocation leave.

Don't you mean embarkation leave?

No, it's something you rub on. He had a sore back.

We were giggling…

He was in this pub in Windsor and he heard singing coming from the Public Bar. Cos they had a piano in there. He said, who's that angel singing? I swear I could marry such a one! So he goes into the Public Bar and there at the piano is this big hairy tattooed sailor singing falsetto. So my dad – being true to himself – said was that you singing just now? And the sailor answered, it was yes. Why? Well that gave my dad a bit of a dilemma. But once he'd made up his mind that was it and he was just about to propose to the matelot when my mum comes out of the toilet and he discovers it was her singing before. So that's how they got together. Then off he goes to India for three and a half years. But he wrote passionate letters home regularly…

To the sailor? Asked Peter.

We don't really know, do we? Anyway Alf Slynne thought he had a chance to get in there – during my dad's absence – to press his suit.

It still needs pressing, said Peter. Did you notice?

Yes. But my mum you see – she had an eye to the main chance for dad who was a handsome sort of Ronald Coleman type and while in India promoted to sergeant. But Dad had a stroke while away and it had pulled his face down a bit one side so he said to Mum when he got back do you still want me? And she took one look at him and said yes so dad borrowed five pounds from a pal for the wedding and – oh look you can drop me off here, Peter! I can catch the tube.

I jumped out of the car. See you tomorrow at the recording, I said…

* * * * *

There follows another sketch I wrote for *IDIOT WEEKLY*. This sketch of a character conflicted and wrestling with himself came years before Peter Sellers created the same sort of character in *Doctor Strangelove* – or *How I Came To Love The Bomb.*

"MORONS WEEKLY" sketch

REPORTER / *Peter Sellers.*

REPORTER:
Good afternoon. I'm from the Morons Weekly… Steps out and in again.
The Morons Weekly sent me along as well.
WIFE:
Oh… won't you come in.
REPORTER:
Both of us?
WIFE:
Do come in… let me take your coat.

WIFE takes his overcoat. She doesn't see he has another one underneath.

REPORTER:
May I take my coat off...
He takes his coat off.
REPORTER:
Nice place you've got here... I like your green curtains.
WIFE:
Yes, they are rather nice.
REPORTER:
I don't care for your green curtains.
WIFE:
They're just up temporarily, while the red ones are at the cleaners.
REPORTER:
Really? Seems a shame when these match the room so nicely.
WIFE:
Would you care for a cup of tea?
REPORTER:
Oh, thank you.
Sits under table.
Wife hesitates, then joins him.
WIFE:
Sugar?
REPORTER:
Two lumps, please.
WIFE:
Two lumps...
REPORTER:
And two for me.
WIFE:
Four lumps?
REPORTER:
What of?
WIFE:
Sugar.
REPORTER:
No, thank you, I take saccharine. Well now, this is very pleasant. Let me ask you a few questions then. No, Roger, let me ask the questions today. You asked them yesterday, Hilary... Roger, I am tired of being baulked and frustrated by your continual criticism... and the looks you've been giving my wife lately... She'll be mine one day... You cad. If you lay a finger on her...

You don't know how to treat a woman…
He rolls out from under the table, fighting himself. Gets up and dusts himself down.
He won't give you any trouble. Well, I'll be off.

REPORTER exits as husband enters. Kisses wife.

HUSBAND:
Hello, luv.
WIFE:
Nice day at the office, dear…
HUSBAND:
Yes, I…
Looks down on floor. Reacts as if someone is lying there…
How long have we been taking lodgers?

Fade.

* * * * *

I co-wrote two Goon Show scripts with Spike Milligan, THE SPON PLAGUE and THE GREAT STATUE DEBATE. That would be before the Goons arrived on TV with IDIOT WEEKLY and subsequently A SHOW CALLED FRED.

Before I arrived on the scene Spike had created a character which he played in The Goon Show called Count Jim Moriarty, a criminal mastermind who became a snivelling wreck and sidekick to Peter Sellers playing Hercules Grytpype-Thynne. I mention this, not to explain the following scene…

* * * * *

BAKER STREET. THE FLAT OF SHERLOCK HOMES AND DR WATSON.

WATSON:
My dear Holmes, I am rather concerned about your state of mind. We have not had a new case for some time now and such genius as you entertain does need employment.

HOLMES:
(Smoking his long stemmed pipe reflectively)
There is a case, Watson, that I am minded to investigate. It is a matter of tracking down the elusive fiend, Moriarty. He has been under cover for some time which does concern me. However Moriarty has recently cropped up in a thing called The Goon Show. As we are currently without a case to occupy us we might look into this strange manifestation of our arch-enemy – this Machiavellian mastermind and his deceits.

WATSON:
No no, my dear Holmes! Desist, if you please! Such is not for us to find Moriarty there, believe me. The Goon Show? I have heard of this crazy show. The Goon Show, yes, my goodness gracious! Do we really want to become entangled with Goons? There is a madness in the bomb happy world of Milligan that could infect us both. I have studied this man. He came back from the war shell-shocked. Instead of seeking medical treatment which he should have done he became a comedy writer.

HOLMES:
It is you that fear infection, my good doctor. I am beyond the world of people's minds, including mine own. Which I observe but do not tamper with. It is our own minds that are the infection, Watson. They give us an identity and with that the fear of oblivion.

WATSON:
I see, yes. We will speak of it no more. Please play your violin, Holmes. Play again Beethoven's unfinished symphony.

HOLMES:
Beethoven found great difficulty in not finishing it, Watson. His wife had to restrain him on several occasions because it was his habit to finish his symphonies and he wanted to but she would not let him.

WATSON:
Nevertheless, please play Holmes. It will smooth the vibrations that interpenetrate and disturb our atmosphere.

HOLMES picks up his violin and begins to play…

* * * * *

THE CASE OF THE RINGING TELEPHONE

One fine day I entered the premises at 9 Orme Court for another writing session with Spike Milligan. Seated behind the reception desk was Janet. She wore a Pixie hat and greeted me cheerfully.

Good-morning, John. You are well as I can see but Spike is locked in his office today and not taking any calls.

He phoned me last night to come in for a writing session, I informed her.

Janet confided, He slept in his office last night.

Thanks Janet, I replied. I saw that the door of Spike's agent, opposite, was closed. How's Norma today?

She's turned into a pillar of salt, replied Janet. I warned her not to look back.

It's something we all have to bear in mind, I said.

I trudged up the stairs to the first floor landing. Hanging on Spike's office door was the sign,

> **DO NOT DISTURB.**
>
> **I AM ALREADY DISTURBED.**

I tapped on the door. It's me! I called out.

No it's not, came the answer. I'm Me! You're confused! I heard Spike unlock the door. He opened it a crack and an unshaven face peered out at me. I could smell turpentine from inside.

Come in, John.

I entered Spike Milligan's office. Yes, there was a painting on an easel, a palate and brushes nearby. The work was wild and worthy of the Summer Academy Exhibition in my opinion. Spike's hair stood awry and he had that Van Gogh asylum at Aix En Provence look but there were no ears lying around on the floor so it was not going to be that bad a day. Bedding was stowed away in a corner. Music flowed into the room. It was Antonio Vivaldi's Storm from *The Four Seasons*. I felt I would shortly be joining Spike in his madness. He turned the record player off.

If you go and get some jam doughnuts, said Spike, I'll tell Janet to make us tea. Spike was thawing out. Good sign.

As the doughnuts gave us a sugar high we got into the work. The lines started coming and we were even laughing at our efforts, it was turning into a good writing session.

I think she's having an affair with a man who is only four foot eleven, he explained. I only stay married for the kids. And of course I'm taller.

How does that help? I asked.

It helps, he said, because I can see over the garden fence. Children are magical, he explained. They're a different species from us. The trouble is, they eventually turn into another set of bloody awful adults and there's nothing we can do about it. They are beautiful butterflies that turn into caterpillars. Nature has got it the wrong way round.

There are worlds within, I said.

Spike stared at me. If you're a mystic, you could live on top of a pole. I bought a house for our family, didn't I? I furnished it with loving care. Antiques – tiles – stained glass rescued from building sites as the property developers are demolishing anything beautiful in London that the Luftwaffe forgot to bomb. I made a beautiful home for the wife and kids and I'm reduced to living in the office, aren't I? I'm a refugee like half the world is. I got out of Finchley with what sanity I had left so that I can work to keep the whole thing going. June is holding my kids hostage in that house. What would you do?

Wait it out, Spike. Nobody's that good or that bad. Things will change.

They can't change for the worse that's for sure, said Spike.

And on we wrote. The day was brightening and Spike might even make up with his wife June and return to Finchley by the end of the day. I liked June. I could not imagine that she was having an affair but then what did I know?

Then the phone rang.

Spike did not immediately answer it though I could see him becoming tense as we applied ourselves to producing the next funny line. It might have been better to take a break and to answer the phone but it was not something I thought wise to suggest. It had to play out. It was like a battle of minds. Who was this telephone intruder at the other end of the line who dared to interrupt our precious writing session? And to cast the fragile mood of Spike so rapidly back into manic?

Was it The Spon Plague, a Goon Show script we were working on? Or The Great Statue Debate? I do not recall.

What I do remember is the interminable sound of the phone (I can still hear it ringing). The receiving instrument had only a few days earlier been re-installed after Spike had the week before wrenched it from its socket and thrown it out of the door, yelling, THE TELEPHONE IS AN INSTRUMENT FROM HELL!! DAMN THE GPO FOR BEING THE NEW INQUISITION!!

Or so it had been reported to me. The last time I had been in with Spike writing there was a GPO telephone engineer crouched in the corner of his office re-installing the phone. This was nothing new. It added to the lustre of the legend of an erratic genius, The Milligan who could well match the fantastic tales told by the other Arch Goon, Peter Sellers.

The phone continued to ring. The other entity, whoever, whatever, was not about to give in. I was tempted to say, Shall I answer it, Spike? How long could this torture go on? Suddenly Milligan lunged across the room, grabbed the ringing phone and yanked it from the socket (in those days it was wired in and this act was irrevocable without calling in the GPO who might take days or even weeks to arrive to rewire it into the socket.) Spike had done it again. Pirouetting gracefully as if choreographed by the great Diaghilev he had thrown the instrument out of the office window which fortunately was open.

That's one way to deal with it, I said. Is that a direct line? A number you only give out to a few people?

It was, he said. Yes.

So it would have been a friend? Or family?

They are all tormentors – friends, family – they all want to make me ill.

I'm a friend. I don't want to make you ill, Spike.

Then don't phone me.

Sometimes you ask me to…

Spike looked pained. John, they want me to go back to the mental hospital with the clanging dustbins in the stairwell. Don't you understand?

OK, Spike, this is just silly. It's done. You've destroyed your personal phone line so… I understand. We can get on. You don't have to get it repaired this time. You can get all your calls through the switchboard downstairs. Monitored by Janet according to your instructions. Whatever suits you, Spike. Win, win!

Peace. Peace suits me, John. Peace and quiet. And Vivaldi. And painting. And writing – writing with you – so let's get on with it…

It was then I noticed something peculiar. From outside in the courtyard by the dustbins came a sound, the plaintive ringing of a telephone.

Listen, I said. The telephone. It's still ringing.

That's impossible, said Spike. The connection is broken.

True, I said. It is technically impossible because it was a wired-in connection that you brutally broke when with superhuman strength you pulled it off the wall. Look! The connecting box is broken! What more proof do you want?

The phone was still ringing outside.

Spike had a strange look in his eyes. Go on, he said. Have you an explanation?

Yes, well… Since you worked on the restoration of the fairy tree Spike in Kensington Palace Gardens you said you've seen a gnome dancing on your picture rail. This could be another peculiar event. A sort of magical beyond our normal understanding thing.

I can't continue my life with that phone ringing, said Spike. I would rather end it. This event does not mean John that I have become wedded to the underworld of gnomes fairies and goblins. It is the fault of the bastard on the other end of the line. Such is the intensity of their desire to destroy my peace of mind. OK we'll settle this once and for all. Come on! Come with me…

We left the office and trooped down the main stairs carpeted in red. Janet, the receptionist, greeted us, Good morning magical Spike! What spells are upon you today, sir?

That's enough, Janet. I cannot play games today. I am having trouble with the real world.

The material world will always end in trouble, she said. I prefer not to live there. Can I help you, Spike?

Do you have the key to the outside door in the basement?

It's hanging on a hook near the door in the basement. Only I would not advise you to go down there, Spike. It will spell trouble.

I'm good at spelling. I can look up trouble in the dictionary if I need to. Thank you. How is your mother, Janet?

She died five years ago, Spike.

Did I came to the funeral?

I wasn't working here then.

Pity. I would have come of course.

Thank you, said Janet.

Is your father still alive?

Yes…

I'll come to his funeral, said Spike.

I'll tell him, she said. He'll be so pleased. Though Dad's very well at the moment.

I can't help that, Janet, said Spike. Where is Norma?

She's turned into a pillar of salt.

I see. Come along, John.

We moved to the stairs that led to the basement. I was first descending the stairs but half way down I stopped. Hang on, I said. Spike, are we being too impulsive?

Spike sat down on a step. What do you mean?

I mean are we being impelled by a narrative not of our own making? I came here today to write with you and yet here we are half way down to the basement.

Spike rubbed his eyes as if he would see clearly with inner vision. He said, Yes, we can stay here and reflect awhile. I agree we must not be rushed. But the phone...

I sat on the step below him.

Is this not the chance to make it a day of love, Spike? Before we go any further? I left Sandhurst – the Royal Military Academy – because I didn't want to kill people.

Spike said, I'm writing to a German Para who was trying to kill me at El Alamein. He was on the exact ridge that we were attacking. I tracked him down after the war. We keep in touch. I was trying to kill him, he was trying to kill me. But it wasn't personal. Not like with the Inland Revenue. They don't only want all my money they want to destroy me so that I cannot make any income so we all go down together. Now that is personal.

I said, That's a nice story about your German Paratrooper pen pal. Was he a Nazi?

I don't know. He's coming to London soon to see me.

Is he dropping by parachute into your back garden in Finchley? He could be a fascist fanatic – one of those that believe Hitler is still alive in South America selling his sperm – Genuine Third Reich Sperm, Guaranteed for One Thousand Years...

The Milligan smiled, a ray of sunlight through his weariness. I love you John you know that. I want the best for you. You're young you will suffer I can't stop that happening. He stood up. Let us continue our journey down the steps.

Are you sure?

There is no turning back. Come on. Spike fixed me with his Irish eyes. One day when you are in mental hospital, John, and you think that nobody cares, I will write to you. That's a promise.

(And Spike did. He kept the promise. He wrote me a beautiful letter when he discovered I was in a psychiatric ward in Edinburgh. To get more idea of that hospital experience you could read CAPTAIN OATES' LEFT SOCK / publisher Samuel French)

* * * * *

BAKER STREET. THE FLAT OF SHERLOCK HOLMES.

Sherlock Holmes is putting on his cape.

WATSON:
Where are you going, Holmes?

HOLMES:
We. Where are we going? We are entering a story, Watson. Of which the Earth is full. No story no Earth.

WATSON:
You mean we have a new case? I would welcome that.

HOLMES:
Our cases are but stories, my dear Watson. And all stories have been already written. We are merely retracing our footsteps.

WATSON
(As he follows Holmes out of the flat)
I must say I don't understand that but it's time we got out into the world and inhaled some fresh air to clear our heads of giddy ideas like that Goon Show emanation of Moriarty! We can forget that one…

* * * * *

Spike entered the basement. I followed. An insistent sound greeted us from outside. The phone is still ringing, I said. We could return to your office and forget all about it. That might be best…

Spike reacting to the pulsating RING RING RING began panting like a hounded deer. No John, we cannot return. We must do what we came to do. Someone is getting at me. And I'm going to find out who that bastard is!

He tried the door to the outside area. It was locked as expected. It had panels of frosted glass that he was trying to peer through. There's somebody out there, he said. Maybe not. You can't tell through this mottled glass...

There is a shadow, I confirmed. It could be from the tree in the street. Hang on – the key's got to be around somewhere. I looked along the walls where it was supposed to be hanging.

Don't bother. Spike wrapped his fist in the sleeve of his cardigan preparing to smash the glass pane in the door.

Found it, I called out in time. I spied the key hanging on a hook just like Janet had said.

Hurry up, said Spike, Whoever that swine is ringing me I'm going to follow him to the ends of the earth and destroy him. It could be that tax inspector who's got my file.

I took the key and unlocked the door. Spike shouldered me aside bursting into the small yard and started moving dustbins around and clanging the lids.

Where's that blasted phone? It fell by the dustbins – it's gone!
BANG! CLANG!

The lids were pulled off and slammed back onto the bins. I followed him into the outside area – hardly a yard – room for the dustbins and concrete steps leading up to the street. We could still hear the phone ringing but where was it coming from? Spike picked up a bin and overturned it, the contents scattering on the ground. He slammed the bin down again.

Spike, steady on!

Spike was looking like Michael Bentine onstage at the Windmill Theatre doing his mad professor act between the nude tableaux vivants.

It could be my mother phoning from Australia! Or my father phoning about my mother! Or my mother phoning about my father! How the hell do I know?

The ringing noise is coming from the street, I said. Someone's taken the phone. Probably heard it ringing and decided to investigate. As it was a chucked out item by the dustbins they decided it was OK to take it...

Spike crossed to the concrete steps ascending to the street. I followed as he climbed and went through the iron gate to the pavement. In time to see a shadowy figure climbing into the back of a taxi holding the phone, the wire dangling. It was still ringing...

STOP! Yelled Spike. Stop that telephone!

The back door of the cab slammed shut as it drew away from the curb and gathered speed down the street,

Spike turned on me. You know who that was? Getting into the cab with my private line?

Hard to tell – it was so all so quick – he was wearing a hat and a raincoat...

Of course! Spike had the glint of madness in his eyes. It was the master of disguises – PETER SELLERS!

Hang on, I said. How could it be that Peter Sellers would be passing by when you happened to throw your telephone out by the basement dustbins? That is too much of a coincidence in anybody's book.

John, you don't know how his mind works...

It's your mind, Spike, that could be making this up. I mean it's got to be rubbish. I laughed to defuse the situation.

Rubbish eh? The Milligan's Mini was parked nearby. He had his car keys in his hands and he was already hurrying over to the car. Are you coming or not?

Deep breath. I followed and jumped in as Spike hardly waiting for me to shut the door gunned away from the curb...

* * * * *

Here we take a Peter Sellers (Idiot Weekly) commercial break :

Peter is holding up a stained white sheet.

Are you having trouble getting rid of laundry stains in your weekly wash? Stains that defeat all your attempts to wash away?

He cuts a hole in a sheet removing the stain and peers through...

Scissors! Use scissors! Buy a pair of scissors today and remove those ugly stains! SCISSORS...!

* * * * *

As he darted in and out of the traffic I said, no sign of the taxi. If you ask me it's a long shot Spike going to the Sellers residence. We don't know that it's him who took the phone. In fact you have to say it's exceedingly unlikely...

What you don't know, John, is that at the Goon Show recording the Sunday before last I told Sellers that if it wasn't for the words that we sweated out every week he'd still being doing the Music Halls.

The Music Halls are closing down, I ventured.

Yes, and I told Sellers he'd be pulled down like them and rebuilt as an office block which would suit his character and if it wasn't for the Goon Show scripts he'd be at the Finchley Labour exchange! So he got nasty and threatened to walk out of the series. I let the producer sort it out. Just because he's got a couple of film parts he imagines he's a Hollywood star.

I did notice that you weren't speaking to each other at the recording last Sunday.

Spike was driving fast as he continued the conversation. The Peter Sellers level of conversation is Princess Margaret that tells you something! He's a brown nosed Royal Crawler! By appointment!

WATCH OUT SPIKE!

We narrowly avoided a fruit barrow which overturned spilling produce onto the road.

Did you see that?

Yes, John. Don't worry. I didn't run over the bananas I'm a vegetarian I care!

Could you slow down, please?

Milligan hit the breaks and slowed to about ten miles an hour which got traffic hooting behind us.

Will that do you, John?

Not far behind in an old Austin followed Watson at the wheel, beside him seated Sherlock Holmes sucking on his pipe...

HOLMES:
Well done, Watson. You're not losing them. But don't get too close.

WATSON:
Are you sure we are in the right story, Holmes? Surely we deserve better than this?

HOLMES:
Patience, my dear Doctor Watson. Patience.

WATSON:
I would like some patients. I don't know why I lost my practice.

HOLMES:
It dissolved.

WATSON:
Dissolved? My practice dissolved? Holmes, I confess I do not understand.

HOLMES:
Watson my dear fellow there is a need to accept after which understanding may or may not come. Why are we stopped?

WATSON:
There is some sort of impediment to our progress. Yes, as far as I can make out it's temporary. It's a sketch, by Jove!

HOLMES:
A sketch?

WATSON:
Yes, we will have to go round it.

HOLMES:
Absolutely, Watson. We are not sketch material! Heaven forfend! Reverse, reverse! Take that side street, Watson!

WATSON reverses the Austin car and accelerates up a side street.

* * * * *

"THE TELEPHONE SKETCH".
(Another sketch Peter liked to play, of course with Graham Stark.)

PETER SELLERS ON PHONE. HE TALKS IN A VERY AFFECTED CULTURED VOICE.

PETER:
Hello… Is that Hermione?

CUT TO GIRL ON PHONE. SHE ALSO TALKS IN A VERY AFFECTED WAY.

GIRL:
Speaking.

CUT FROM ONE TO THE OTHER AS THEY SPEAK.

PETER:
Well, I'm Rodney... you don't know me... but a mutual friend gave me your phone number...
GIRL:
Oh, that was naughty...
PETER:
I know... I know it's naughty... but, well, I wondered... would you like to come out to dinner this evening?
GIRL:
Well really... it is naughty of you.
PETER:
I know it's naughty.
GIRL:
It is...
PETER:
I know...
GIRL:
Well, alright...
PETER:
Oh, splendid... I'll pick you up at seven...bye bye...
GIRL:
Bye bye...

CUT BACK TO PETER HANGING UP.

PETER:
In a very common voice. Wonderful what a bit of the old posh chat'll do...

CUT TO GIRL ALSO HANGING UP.

GIRL:
Also terribly common. Now what clobber shall I put on for this Charlie tonight.

<u>END OF SKETCH</u>

* * * * *

WATSON:
We are back en-route, Holmes. It was a minor diversion but I'm afraid we have totally lost the car that we were following.

HOLMES:
I'll give you an address in Finchley, Watson. That's where Peter Sellers lives.

WATSON:
Why would they go there?

HOLMES:
Elementary, my dear Watson. Mr Milligan is motivated by the tides of passion not by logic. There we shall follow.

WATSON:
But what has this to do with Moriarty?

HOLMES:
Possibly nothing, my dear Watson. Possibly everything. For where Moriarty is be sure that great harm is intended…

* * * * *

There are no atheists in cars driven by Spike Milligan. With heartfelt thanks to a God I did not believe in I alighted onto the pavement in Finchley.

We entered a block of flats to be confronted by the concierge. Spike sensed trouble and immediately changed his mood to genial, Hello Lawrence!

Hello, Mr Milligan, sir. We've missed you since you've moved out of the building. It's been very quiet. We haven't had to call the police in once.

Spike said, If you are referring to the incident when I supposedly attacked Mr Sellers with a knife the police officer disarmed me then tackled Mr Sellers himself. I then threw my naked body between the two of them and pleaded for his life. It was all in the Golders Green Morning Post.

I have my copy of it cut out and framed, sir.

It's me that was framed. That's why I moved out of the building.

Why did you attack Mr Sellers naked Mr Milligan? It's never been solved.

Because he refused to give me the name of his tailor. It was a confusing incident, a prank that got out of hand. It's nice to see you again Gunner Biggs. Lawrence here was a Desert Rat. We are old comrades. I carried him out of a minefield...

It wasn't me, Spike.

It will be next time.

Indeed sir. But I must ask you not to take the lift until I have called whoever you wish to visit which I take to be Mr Sellers?

Correct. You have won a fortnight in Bangkok with Dirk Bogarde impersonating Margaret Lockwood. Gunner Biggs, I must ask you not to pick up that telephone.

The concierge had gone behind his desk and was reaching for the phone.

Because it is Mr Sellers' birthday, explained Spike. And I want it to be a surprise.

No it's not, replied the ex-military concierge. I know the birthday of Peter Sellers. It's in my diary.

Well it will be his birthday.

You mean it's a surprise that it's not his birthday?

Precisely.

I'm sorry, Mr Milligan, but for security reasons I must phone the recipient of your intended visit. We have our procedures for the protection of this building from unwelcome visitors. It would be more than my job is worth...

The concierge reached again for the phone...

STOP! Ordered Spike. I am impersonating your overall commander, General Montgomery! Stand at ease chaps! Gather round! Come closer, that's better... Now, I do not want to hear this word again – retreat! In future it is true that we will sometimes be advancing backwards. Right? Got that? Advancing backwards! Good! Very good! Also be aware that Gunner Milligan is on a vital clandestine mission behind enemy lines. He will now give Gunner Biggs a ten pound note towards his crappy pension and as compensation for his war wound – septicaemia caught from scratching himself on a barbed wire entanglement during his advance backwards from El Alamein – before our advance to El Alamein – before we advanced backwards again and then advanced. Advanced, yes... sometimes we go sideways but I will not go into that because I do not want confuse you. Only Rommel do we confuse! Right, now pay attention! You are all ordered to suffer a bout of amnesia and let Gunner Milligan past your post immediately. Is that quite clear? Right chaps! Off you go and good hunting!

Spike placed two five pound notes on the desk. The concierge picked up the notes and tucked them into the pocket of his shoddy blue uniform. He drew himself up and took a deep breath to inflate his uniform, Right gentlemen, you may proceed with caution into No Man's Land. The risk is yours. I haven't seen you. Not at all. Good luck!

We proceeded to the lift.

Fifth floor, said Spike. I used to live with my wife and family on the same floor as Peter Sellers. It was a disaster.

The lift pinged and the doors opened. We walked along the beige carpeting towards the door at the end of the corridor. Spike rang the bell.

I was getting worried. Was this a story from which there was no escaping or was Spike deliberately adding to his own legend? Turning adversity into a golden opportunity for self-publicity? Had he even engineered the seeming impossibility of the ringing telephone and called me to his office to witness the ensuing drama? Surely now we had come to the climax as these two geniuses of comedy, Peter Sellers and Spike Milligan, clashed in this corridor acting out their pantomimes.

Peter opened the door. He was wearing black silk pyjamas and golden slippers. Spike! My, my! What a surprise! Have you come to apologise? Have you? Was your conscience weighing upon you too heavily? I would invite you in but I won't. Ann and the kids have gone to the country to cool off and I'm all on my own. Vulnerable. Very Vulnerable. Not knowing your state of mind – whether it's savage or – or contrite. I don't want you smashing the place up. I would remind you, Spike, there is a restraining order on you regarding this building so you obviously bribed your way in past our corrupt concierge. Oh hello John! And goodbye everyone!

Sellers tried to close the door but Milligan placed his foot in the way.

Remove your foot from my premises. You are trespassing, hissed Sellers. Shouldn't you be back at the office writing next Sunday's Goon Show? That should be occupying your mind not this criminal intrusion into my privacy. Spike's foot remained stuck inside the door. Peter continued in a more reasonable vein, not that Spike had ever delivered a Goon Show script that is not absurdly funny. All his failings lie elsewhere. If you could persuade him that his jealousy for my incredible luck in the film industry is not my fault – and that where I go he cannot follow – that is to international fame and Hollywood. Yes, I would be most grateful if you could get that across to him, John. Spike's future lies essentially behind him, with the BBC. And while you have ears to listen, Spike, I would remind you that you are banned from this building. You were depreciating the property prices when you and the outcome of your loins lived here along the corridor with your odd habits of reproduction – throwing chicken bones into the corridor...

That wasn't me, said Spike. I'm a vegetarian. I would only throw a live chicken into the corridor for you to kill later.

Please, Spike, get your foot out of my doorway. I have given enough hospitality to your foot. I confess, mate, I feel sorry for you.

Spike said hoarsely, could I have a glass of water?

Certainly. Hang on...

Peter left us standing on his threshold as he disappeared inside the apartment. I said nothing. Spike was panting like a tired dog. Was he gathering himself for the tumult? Peter returned with a glass of water and handed it to Spike. We waited while Spike downed the glass of water to the last drop and handed the empty glass back to his fellow goon.

Thanks.

Will that be all then?

Yes. Thank you. I will not join you in a slanging match, Peter, it would be far too easy. Instead I will bless you with love and light.

Spike looked tired, beaten, but not unhappy.

I do not need your hand-me-down one size fits all blessing, said Peter. I have enough love in my life and the light I get from the Electricity Board.

Nevertheless the blessing remains, said Spike.

Well thanks. See you Sunday. Sellers shut his front door. We turned, Spike and I, and trudged back to the lift.

You didn't mention the phone, I said.

It's not him, said Spike. You were right. I shouldn't be here. I am humiliated as was Matt Talbot the Irish working class Saint. Do you know about him?

No...

I must welcome the experience. It's worth more than any victory. Now let's get back to Bayswater and get on with the script, John.

So this was the Saint Spike version born out of suffering. I felt somehow privileged to witness it. It was then we heard a phone ringing – a familiar plaintiff bleat but then that could be said of any distant phone seeking a receiver. Spike stopped in his tracks,

Listen?

That could be any phone, Spike.

Don't be a bloody fool. Do you think I don't know my own telephone when it rings? He turned and strode back to the Sellers front door. The noise of the phone was louder so it was probably was coming from inside the Arch Goon's flat. Spike savaged the bell with his finger keeping it jammed upon the button. Peter flung open the door.

Well?

That is my telephone you've got in there. Spike spoke quietly. I accept that you might be possessed Peter of black magic that allows you to put spells on my telephone. He became louder. I demand you let me answer my own telephone!

Are you mad, Milligan? Should you be hospitalised? Perhaps put to sleep for a week. It worked last time. What are you raving on about? Do go home.

Let me through, damn you! Spike's temper was rising as the phone ringing continued. Let me answer my phone! Do you think I don't recognise it? It could be my mother phoning that my father has died – or visa versa how do I know? It could be a family emergency. For the last time stand aside Sellers. All thought of sainthood was gone as Spike grappled with his fellow Goon to gain entrance to the household...

Go away, you mad crazy fool! Peter pushed back. Unhand me, you hear? You have the devil in you. Let go of my black silk Japanese Harrods pyjamas bought in the January Sales or I'll call the police! Police! Or better still, a priest! A priest to have you exorcised!

The two Goons were struggling in the doorway.

Spike grunted, It is you that has contact with the underworld – you and your seances – and you that have conjured up a spirit to infect my phone – my personal phone! Let me through!

Stop, Milligan! Do I have to resort to judo? This is an official warning.

The phone somewhere inside the flat continued to ring. Spike succeeded in shoving Peter to the floor. The Milligan rushed into the bowels of the flat. The crumpled Sellers proclaimed dramatically, I am wounded! Possibly not mortally but then we are all one breath away from eternity. I helped Peter to his feet and we entered the flat following Spike into the lounge in time to see him across the spacious room snatching up the phone.

Yes?... What?... Who?... When?... Very well... Yes, I'll write it down... Milligan picked up a pencil and wrote some details on a pad that lay by the receiver. Then he said, Yes, I'll make sure he gets it. He hung up the receiver and tore the page from the pad.

He handed it to Peter...

It's your dentist. He confirms that he can see you on Thursday afternoon at three-thirty for a cleaning.

Peter said, Thank you, Spike. As you're here would you fancy a coffee? It's brewing. And I've got some rather lovely bagels in the fridge – salmon and soft cheese from my local Jewish deli.

Thank you, said Spike. I would enjoy a circumcised bagel. Do you mind if I sit down?

By all means. Try one of the chairs. I bought them last week from Heals, Tottenham Court Road, where I bumped into Alec Guinness of all people.

Spike sank into one of the post modern Scandinavian chairs. How was Alec Guinness? He enquired.

I think he has trouble returning to himself after his part. He was in tropical gear. I know we've had a heat wave recently but he is still passing himself off as Colonel Nicholson in *The Bridge Over The River Kwai*.

Spike said, The sooner the monsoon breaks the better for all of us. The heat, the flies, the native girls!

They both laughed.

What joy to hear them as if never a cross word had passed between them. The storm had passed and the two Arch Goons were restored to friendship. They had both enjoyed the drama and in my humble opinion played it to the hilt. It had purged their friendship and the tale would be told in many ways over the coming months enhancing both their reputations for genius and eccentricity. Milligan was struck off Sellers' shit list for the time being and the following Sunday at the Camden Theatre the recording of The Spon Plague went down like a bomb with the audience. Everyone was happy, including Harry Secombe, but then he was never unhappy, was he?

The following Thursday we were in another writing session. A GPO engineer was crouched in the corner of the office installing a new telephone. We were back in business. There was one incident, perhaps worth a mention. I am not quite sure when it was but Spike and I were taking a walk together in Bayswater to have a break and buy some jam doughnuts and as we walked past a public red telephone box the phone was ringing. Spike stopped, a strange look on his face. He returned to the telephone box and entered shutting the door. He picked up the receiver. I could not hear what was said but eventually he put the receiver down and returned to the street. It was my mother, he said. From Australia. She's well. She been trying to get hold of me for ages. We entered the bakers shop and bought six jam doughnuts and then strolled back to the office meanwhile tossing ideas back and forth trying to think of another absurd story for the Goon Show.

As we walked away Holmes and Watson appeared and approached the red telephone box. The telephone started ringing. Watson opened the red door intent on answering the call. No! Commanded Sherlock Holmes. Stand back, Watson! For God's sake! As Watson let go of the door and stepped back the telephone exploded...

WATSON:
My God, you were right, Holmes. What caused that?

HOLMES:
Elementary, my dear Watson, that call was meant for Mr Milligan. I managed to delay it by getting a call from his mother diverted to the telephone box – don't ask me how. Let us say it is a revision to the text. The delay doubtless saved his life...

WATSON:
But who would play such a dastardly trick upon this comedic writer?

HOLMES:
It had to come, Watson. Mr Milligan has been using the character of Moriarty in his Goon Shows presenting him as a gibbering fawning fool. This was Moriarty's attempt at revenge.

WATSON:
Good Heavens! That's rather brilliant deduction, Holmes. Well done I must say. The Revenge Of Moriarty, we might call it! Surely though he will not stop at one attempt?

HOLMES:
I cannot say. We are once more in a story not of our own making. We attempt to act in surprising ways, not necessarily in character. Come along, Watson. Let us be going. We shall leave this story though it may seek us out further...

They leave the scene of the smouldering telephone box.

WATSON:
Remarkable! Quite remarkable! In future, Holmes, I will think twice before I question your commitment to a case. I will indeed. But who actually took the ringing telephone from the dustbin area?

HOLMES:
It had to be Moriarty to further his fiendish plot. To spread discord and havoc between Mr Milligan and Mr Sellers – another Goon who has been mocking him every week on the Goon Show. For now Count Moriarty is foiled.

WATSON:
Ah, Yes, Yes. Brilliant, Holmes! Well done and so home for tea…

* * * * *

Peter Sellers and Spike Milligan sing and dance in bottomless dustbins accompanied by the Edwardian Evening Of British Rubbish Alberts on their brass instruments. Spike has now taken over as editor in chief of scripts as we move to a second series of Goon humour on television, now retitled,

A SHOW CALLED FRED

When you're blue and low down
Don't get into a trance
Just jump into a dustbin and dance!
Throw away your rubbish!
Show them you don't care!
When they come to empty it,
It won't be there…
When you're tired and weary
And life has lost romance
Jump into a dustbin and dance, dance, DANCE!

* * * * *

CAPTION – "A DAY IN HYDE PARK" Orchestra: music

<u>Park Set</u>: BENCH CENTRE STAGE WITH BUSHES BEHIND IT. GRAHAM STROLLS ON IN 17TH CENTURY COSTUME. SITS DOWN ON BENCH. UNROLLS SCROLL AND STARTS READING IT. PETER, WEARING 20TH CENTURY CIVIL SERVICE TYPE CLOTHES, COMES ON READING NEWSPAPER. SITS NEXT TO GRAHAM WITHOUT NOTICING HIM.

PETER:
Tut… tut… tut… things get worse every day… the country's going to the dogs.
GRAHAM:
Indeed yes – another economic crisis on the way, I fear.
PETER:
No doubt about it. I mean you've only got to take the cost of living these days.
GRAHAM:
Shocking. Do you know that the rent I pay for my house has gone up to five shillings a month.
PETER:
Oh, it's terrible I… how much?
GRAHAM:
Five shillings a month – it's sheer highway robbery.
PETER:
There's no doubt about that… still if you can get away with it…
GRAHAM:
What do you mean?
PETER:
Do you realise that I pay 20 pounds a month for a flat?
GRAHAM:
A flat what?

LOOK OF SUSPICION COMES TO PETER'S FACE. SLOWLY THEY TURN AND LOOK AT EACH OTHER. SURPRISED BUSINESS TURNING TO LAUGHTER AT EACH OTHER'S APPEARANCE.

GRAHAM:
It's quite absurd – like a dream…
PETER:
A dream – that's it – this is all a dream.
GRAHAM:
Oh… yes, of course… thank goodness for that. But I've never had a dream like this before.
PETER:
That's because… it's _my_ dream.
GRAHAM:
Oh… I see… wait a minute… if this is your dream… then I only exist because _you_ are dreaming about me.

PETER:
Yes… that's right…
GRAHAM:
And when… and when you wake up… I disappear.
PETER:
Mmmmmmm…
GRAHAM:
That is… I cease to exist…
PETER:
Yes…
GRAHAM:
It's my dream.
PETER:
It is not.
GRAHAM:
Get out!
PETER:
What?
GRAHAM:
Get out of my dream!
PETER:
You have the audacity to tell me to get out of my own dream.
GRAHAM:
It's my dream…
PETER:
It is not… this dream is mine… I know it is… I always dream when I have cheese for supper.
GRAHAM:
You didn't have cheese for supper.
PETER:
I did.
GRAHAM:
No… you thought you had cheese for supper… yes… because I dreamt you had cheese for supper.
PETER:
No… you dreamt I had cheese for supper… yes… because I dreamt that you dreamt that I had cheese for supper.
GRAHAM:
No… you dreamt that I dreamt that you had cheese for supper yes… yes…

because… I dreamt that you dreamt that I was dreaming that I… that I… that I… that I had cheese for supper.
PETER:
But *you* didn't have cheese for supper.
GRAHAM:
Oh… I wondered why I felt so hungry.
PETER:
So, it's my dream.
GRAHAM:
I suppose it is.
PETER:
Well, I can't stand here chatting to you… for ever. I'm going to pinch myself now and wake up…
GRAHAM:
Oh no… you can't do that… you've forgotten… when you wake up… I disappear…
PETER:
I hadn't forgotten – goodbye…
GRAHAM:
Turning away and covering his eyes. No… you can't do this to me… no…

PETER DOES WAKING UP BUSINESS. NOTHING HAPPENS. PETER GOES UP TO GRAHAM AND TAPS HIM ON THE SHOULDER.

PETER:
My dear fellow…
GRAHAM:
You haven't…
PETER:
I couldn't…
GRAHAM:
Couldn't…?
PETER:
Couldn't bring myself to leave you…
GRAHAM:
Oh, you are kind – if I'd have been you I know I would have woken myself up… I would… like this… Goes to pinch himself.
PETER:
Don't ! Don't do that ! You'll make me disappear…

GRAHAM:
Eh?
PETER:
I mean… you'll… you'll…
GRAHAM:
Oh… you did try and wake yourself up… but it didn't work – because it's my dream, isn't it?
PETER:
Yes.
PETER:
Ha… ha… ha… look at you… dressed up as though you're in the seventeenth century… ha… ha… ha…
GRAHAM:
He… he… he… as though… as though… what century do you think we're in then… ha… ha… ha.
PETER:
Ha… ha… ha… what do you mean… the twentieth, of course… ha… ha… ha…
GRAHAM:
The seventeenth you mean… ha… ha… ha…
PETER:
The twentieth… ha.
GRAHAM:
The seventeenth… ah huh…

PETER WITH SMILE FROZEN ON HIS FACE.

PETER:
The twentieth…

GRAHAM LAUGHS, DRIES AND SMILES.

GRAHAM:
Freezing. The seventeenth.

THEIR SMILES TURN TO APPREHENSION.

PETER:
This is today's newspaper… read the date…

Hands Graham paper.
GRAHAM:
This is today's news scroll... acquaint yourself with the motif...
Hands Peter scroll.

They examine the documents with growing apprehension.

PETER:
There's something wrong, isn't there?
GRAHAM:
If you'd had your way I would have been stuck in my own dream for ever, wouldn't I?
PETER:
I didn't mean... any...
GRAHAM:
I've got a wife and seven children, and they'd have no-one to work for if I wasn't there...
PETER:
My dear friend...
GRAHAM:
No – don't you my dear friend me... I'm going to wake myself up now...
PETER:
Oh, please stay... just a little while... I know a wonderful shaggy dog story... There was a knight and one day...
GRAHAM:
It's no good, I've got to wake myself up now anyway or I'll be late for work...
PETER:
No...don't... please... Graham does waking up business... Nothing happens.
PETER:
It's not your dream...
GRAHAM:
It's not yours either...
PETER:
No...
GRAHAM:
Then whose dream is it?

DAVE AS CAVEMAN POKES HIS HEAD THROUGH BUSHES BEHIND BENCH AND GUFFAWS.

PETER:
Oh no…
GRAHAM:
It's… his dream…

DAVE STILL GUFFAWING CLIMBS OVER BENCH. PETER AND GRAHAM GO UP TO HIM CAUTIOUSLY.

GRAHAM:
We… we…
PETER:
We… your friends…

DAVE GIVES BIG GUFFAW.

GRAHAM:
Oh, dear… if he laughs much louder he'll wake himself up.

PETER TAKES WATCH FROM HIS WAISTCOAT.

PETER:
For you… you… very nice…

DAVE LICKS IT AND THROWS IT AWAY IN DISGUST. THEN PUTS HIS HAND AS THOUGH TO PINCH HIMSELF.

GRAHAM:
Look out… he's going to wake himself up… get him… quickly.

THEY TRY AND STOP DAVE BUT HE BREAKS FREE AND DOES WAKING UP BUSINESS. NOTHING HAPPENS. THEY STARE AT EACH OTHER.

PETER:
It's… it's… not him…

GRAHAM:
Then we're safe...
PETER:
Yes...

THEY SIT DOWN ON BENCH WITH RELIEF.

FX : REGULAR SNORING NOISE.
THEY ALL LOOK UP PUZZLED AND APPREHENSIVE.

PETER:
Look !!!

ALL STARE IN HORROR TO WHERE PETER IS POINTING.
CUT TO SHOT OF SLEEPING DOG.
CUT TO SHOT OF TRIO.

GRAHAM:
Loudly. Oh no... not that... I can't bear it... I'm just a bit of a dog's dream... oh no...
PETER:
Ssssssh.... you'll wake him up... and then we'd all be finished.
GRAHAM:
Ooooooooooooh....
PETER:
We must get some sleeping pills...
GRAHAM:
Ah yes... that's the thing... that's the... oh... Sniffs. Oh.... I think I'm going to... to sneeze...
PETER:
You mustn't... you mustn't... you'll wake him up...
GRAHAM:
I... I... I...can't help...help... Gives terrific sneeze.

CUT TO SHOT OF DOG WAKING UP. DOG STRETCHES AND WALKS OFF.

CUT TO ORIGINAL SCENE. THERE ARE THREE SETS OF BONES THERE. ONE HAS SKINS ROUND IT, ONE HAS PETER'S HAT AND UMBRELLA, AND THE OTHER HAS GRAHAM'S HAT ON IT.

PETER:
Voice on echo. You bloody fool !

* * * * *

I am playing squash with Spike. He bounds around energetically hitting the black rubber ball often and beating me more times than I can defeat him. As I had previously played but not a lot at RMA Sandhurst Spike addresses me thus,

Well played Somme Company! You nearly hit the ball then!

I fan the air sometimes, I reply. Because it's getting hot in here. It is a ploy Milligan, to put you off your guard…

We rest awhile slumped against the walls. Hearing the sounds of play from another court, Spike shouts,

KEEP QUIET! THERE ARE PEOPLE TRYING TO SLEEP IN HERE! LEAVE A PINT OF MILK BY THE DOOR AND PISS OFF!

* * * * *

Afterwards we went back to the office in Orme Court. What shall we do, Spike. Let's do nothing, John, that way life happens. Spike's friend Cliff Morgan walked in. Then a well known sports broadcaster, previously the Welsh International Rugby Union fly half. Ohh, he said, my back is playing me up today! How is your front? Asked Spike. It's like the front of Selfridges, said Cliff. Full of wonders that you cannot afford. Have you seen their Christmas windows this year? What a treat they are! It's Easter, said Spike. Cliff laughed. Well there you go, boyo. I'm not one for an argument. I keep my energies for the game. How are you, John? Spike has just beaten me at squash five games to nil, I said. He was lucky to get nil, said Spike. You said that about Ireland last Saturday when they were beaten by England at the rugby at Twickenham, said Cliff Morgan. You said Ireland were lucky to get nil. Spike said, I am recycling a witty line. If you do not laugh then I will not pay for dinner tonight at the Trattoria. Oh, said Cliff, you see that, John. Spike has fallen on hard times. He's bribing us to laugh at his jokes now. It's worth it for a good dinner. If you laugh you'll be invited as well. We laughed. Dinner at the Italian restaurant off High Street Kensington that night was great fun…

* * * * *

Peter Sellers as LORD NIT makes a hilarious rendering of the following sketch, accompanied by Graham Stark...

"LORD NIT – NUMBER PLATE SKETCH".

LORD NIT, IN SHEEPSKIN COAT, WALKS INTO GARAGE :
GARAGE OFFICE,
AS LORD NIT ENTERS. PROPRIETOR DOING OFFICE WORK.

LORD NIT:
Good afternoon. Is my… (Makes car noise – speeding car horn – brakes)… ready yet?

PROP:
Oh, Lord Nit, one moment… (Presses intercom). Hello. Service report on Lord Nit's…
(Hesitates – makes similar car noises into intercom).
Registration number NIT 1.
LORD NIT:
Yes…
PROP:
Won't keep you a moment, me Lord – how did you come by that registration number then?
LORD NIT:
NIT 1 – NIT 1 – yes. (Rubbing his hands together). It did take some tracking down. Actually, I found it in North Wales of all places – on a (Makes animal noises – moo – baa – woof woof).
PROP:
Zoo?
LORD NIT:
No, a farm – a farm in North Wales. There it was – NIT 1. The number plate I'd been searching for – of all things it was on a (Makes chugging noise).
PROP:
Chicken?
LORD NIT:
No – tractor. Yes, I had to buy the tractor to get the number plate. I had to have it…
PROP:
Because you are a NIT?

LORD NIT:
Yes. In fact I had to buy the farm to get the tractor to get the registration number NIT 1 – jolly good, what? A lovely story. Now when I drive in the House of Lords they all know – they say – "Here comes the first Nit of the Land!" NIT 1! Or they might say "Excuse me, constable, where can I see my local MP?" – but that's nothing to do with me, is it? Good show…

MECHANIC (CAN BE A WOMAN) COMES IN WITH REGISTRATION PLATE, NIT 1 AND A FILE. PROPRIETOR OPENS FILE.

PROP:
Oh, dear – well we gave it a good service trial, me Lud…
LORD NIT:
Splendid.
PROP:
On the road – a road trial.
LORD NIT:
Good – yes?
PROP:
And the car came off the number plate.
LORD NIT:
Oh.
PROP:
Yes – you see Lord Nit the car was not securely fixed to the number plate – and it came off.
LORD NIT:
Have you lost it?
PROP:
To Mechanic : Have you lost it? The bit wot's come off?
MECHANIC:
Wot?
PROP:
The car wot come off the back of this number plate – wot happened to it?
MECHANIC:
I lost it… the bolt came off…
PROP:
What was it?
MECHANIC:
It was a three inch…

PROP:
No, no – the car Nigel…
LORD NIT:
Er, what was it – a Silver Cloud Rolls I think it was – I could be mistaken.
PROP:
To Mechanic : 'is Silver Cloud come orf the number plate…
MECHANIC:
Yeah…
PROP:
Well, go and see if we got another one…
MECHANIC:
Right.

MECHANIC EXITS.

PROP:
Don't worry, Lord Nit, we'll soon get you a replacement Rolls Royce.
LORD NIT:
Thank heavens.
PROP:
I'll get it screwed on for you…
LORD NIT:
(Writing out cheque.) How much will that be?
PROP:
Twelve thousand pounds.
LORD NIT:
Right.
PROP:
And, oh, there's a service charge for screwing on the bolts of seventeen and sixpence…
LORD NIT:
How dare you! I'm not paying an exorbitant labour charge like that, my man! Nobody takes advantage of a NIT, I tell you! Where's your mechanic? Where is he? (Mechanic enters with number plate. Lord Nit grabs it). I'll get my number plate serviced elsewhere! Good morning!

LORD NIT EXITS – WITH HIS NUMBER PLATE

* * * * *

Spike Milligan was a champion in the cause of the recognition of bi-polar disease as a mental illness, in those days known as manic-depression. He suffered with this from time to time and was in contact with fellow-sufferers to offer recognition, encouragement and help...

Which does not explain nor need it do so a day of filming in the grounds of an abandoned clinic near London. Spike played himself as a patient which he had been somewhere a few months before and he wanted to see what might happen in a re-creation of a state of mind. I was wearing a white coat and carried a stethoscope around my neck so I was to be the doctor...

DOCTOR:
How are we today, Spike?

SPIKE:
We? We? How many of us are there left, Doctor? Of the we? Since our Division attempted to assault Mount Casino? Right? Is that what you want to know?

DOCTOR:
I love your war books. Hitler, My Part In His Downfall. Funny but compassionate. Let's try again. How are you feeling? Today? Spike?

SPIKE:
How am I feeling? Doctor? What? I don't know how I feel. I pay you to tell me how I feel. That is your job. That is why I'm here – in a private clinic paying – paying for you to tell me how I feel. Please – you tell me because I don't know any more. The explosions have deafened me. We were being mortared by the Germans – that's why I can't stand noise any more.

DOCTOR:
War trauma. Good. It's all coming out. It sounds like you're a little anxious today, Spike. That you are feeling anxious.

SPIKE:
CUT!

DIRECTOR:
OK, stop the camera. That was a good take, Spike. We can use it.

SPIKE:
It's too serious. We're not qualified to deliver these sort of judgements.

DIRECTOR:
You want it more Running, Jumping, Standing Still…? Like a mad patient running past with a big net chasing non-existent butterflies and laughing hysterically?

SPIKE:
No, Jeffry. It's too conventionally unconventional – it's what people expect. Which is next to boring.

DIRECTOR:
OK, Spike. Only we've got the props if you change your mind.

SPIKE:
If I do I'll chase the butterflies! It's about me, right? Chasing caterpillars. Everyone's so busy munching cabbage they don't even imagine for a moment that they could turn into butterflies.

DIRECTOR:
Actually I am still filming on one camera, Spike. So I've got that. That caterpillar rift – brilliant.

SPIKE:
I'm glad you think so. Let's start the scene again, Jeffry. John, you're the Doctor. Can you be more off the wall this time – we can still get to our objective? What is written.

JOHN/ DOCTOR:
OK. Yeah… Can we shoot before I have time to think about it?

DIRECTOR:
Stand by!

RUNNING BOY:
(With clapper board)
Scene 1, Take 2!

DIRECTOR:
Action!

DOCTOR:
There you are, Spike. A tangible asset to the clinic – we're in no hurry to get you well, believe me! Not on the daily rate you are paying, mate! If you want to know, the best chance you have of getting out of here is to go bankrupt – then we'd throw you out.

SPIKE:
Have you considered, Doctor, it is the world that is mad, not me?

DOCTOR:
Yes, but the world cannot afford our fees. You can – at the moment that is. We have done exhaustive tests and established that you are clinically solvent.

SPIKE:
Doctor, why did you put me to sleep for three days?

DOCTOR:
Because the kitchens were being refurbished. Done you the world of good! Look at you! Bouncing with an exuberance which is frankly quite dangerous. Because the only way out is down…

SPIKE:
People can't see psychic pain. They can see broken legs. They understand broken legs. Not broken minds.

DOCTOR:
That's a bit deep for me, Spike. I'm really into magic today and I would say – speaking as a clinician who has spent time working in the African jungle with primitive tribes from whom I learnt more than I could possibly teach them – I would say that someone bears you ill-will. And has probably paid to have a spell put on you.

SPIKE:
Yes, The Inland Revenue. They keep phoning me for money which stops me working to pay them enormous amounts. So I get depressed and pay enormous amounts to come here instead which solves nothing except that I may become well enough to go out and face further persecution.

DOCTOR:
Then you must put a spell on the Inland Revenue, Spike. To neutralise what they are doing to you. If you would care to look in that pond over there – at your reflection – it's magical – and cast a spell – that would put you on the road to recovery.

DIRECTOR:
CUT! Good, good… OK, folks! Let's go to the ornamental pond. Chop, chop! Good work!

SPIKE:
Just shoot while we're walking to the poetry bit at the pond. If it comes out serious – don't think about it – we're on theme…

DIRECTOR:
OK… Keep rolling…

They walk towards the pond.

SPIKE:
Is all this on the National Health? Or are spells Private?

DOCTOR:
We are trying to get the BMA to recognise spells, Spike. Because essentially they are more efficacious than many medicines which – by the way – often work because people believe in them – so there's not much difference is there? Except no diarrhoea side effects…

SPIKE:
And no funny side effects for me at the moment, Doctor, as you've got all the lines. But I like it so let's keep going…

AT THE ORNAMENTAL POND.

CLAPPER BOY:
Scene Two, Take One!

DIRECTOR:
Action!

SPIKE:
Oh pond! Green slimed and froggy spawned
Filth! A pond life still before man's brief morn
From your darting depths a gold fish hovers
From you I crawled and stood to call men brothers
How false they have become
You spawned me when I was One,
Not two or three or crowd or regiment.
Is this why I left the pond to enter in such sentiment?
Now aid me when I call you magic pond
To make my spell into a magic bond!
Speak!

THE POND:
Ask of me what you would have
It shall be so…
In me there is no split
The female and the male is but one lick!
You crawled upon the earth to make it two
And have your fun…
And money you invented and thus crime
It ne'er was so when you were One,
And you were mine…
Content in my green slime…
But I will follow you where you would go
So make your wish or cast your spell
Though you go through the halls of hell
All shall end well….

JOHN:
Do not speak loudly, Spike
Keep your spell
Close to your heart…
Make your vow, it shall end well…
Though as your doctor you be prone to faint
Other scenes appear and scenery the mind paints…

SPIKE:
It shall be so, my spell is made!

Let earth tremble and bodies be afraid
And round and round I go...
Faster yet! I cannot slow...
Twisted by an energy not mine.
Is it the devil? Or that which is Divine?
I spin and spin propelled by hands
Invisible as the music from a magic band...
I fall into a pattern
Call it The Halls Of Hell!
Only Heaven's Angels end this story well...

The spinning Milligan collapsed as the doctor stepped forward applying the stethoscope and checking for a pulse.

DOCTOR:
He is in a faint where we have become unreal to him. We are other, our parts are sundered.

SPIKE (Sitting up):
Hey, you my good fellow! Help me up! Help me up! And tell me? Am I spending a fortnight in Margate with the Prince of Wales? Because I think I won him with an Ernie bond and could be wearing his socks.

JOHN / DOCTOR:
No, that is not so. I am your doctor...

SPIKE:
Never mind that. Bring me my overdraft immediately!

OVERDRAFT:
Coming master...! Coming!

A bedraggled figure appears dragging a chain which is attached to him.

OVERDRAFT:
Coming! Coming! You now owe me three thousand four hundred and sixteen pounds and three pence! I have escaped from the bank vaults to see the light of day and to claim 27% compound interest! Five thousand six hundred and....totally – I have the figures – the amount owed growing as we speak, hahaha...!

SPIKE:
Never mind that! You do not frighten me, you miserable spectre!

OVERDRAFT:
You owe me, Mr Milligan! And I have come to claim! You summoned me – where's your advantage? Money – money – money…

SPIKE:
(Producing a revolver) This is what you get in settlement…

Spike shoots the overdraft dead.

SPIKE:
I enjoyed that…
Thus are my finances transformed,
It is a brighter day,
My overdraft dispatched,
No more those wretched compounds shall I pay.
And banks and bankers now pay heed…
For humanity has a greater need
For figures conjured for their vantage and imagination
Shall no longer be the ruin of our fair nation…

MATRON:
(Approaches, Irish for sure) Ahh, there you are, Mr Milligan, for sure!

SPIKE:
I am not sure it's me, Matron. There lies my ailment. What can I do for you?

MATRON:
That you had better not do, Mr Milligan,
For better men than you have tried!
It's proved to be a bumpy ride!
Now, let us see what's what?
In other words what's left and what is not?
Have you been, Mr Milligan, your privileges abusing?
I will be frank in words that I am using…

SPIKE:
Be not Frank, Matron, but rather Percy,

That in your words I find a mercy...

MATRON:
In Percy then let this be known
Your sanity's departed, to other places flown.
While in this place you have no lovers
And sleep with hands outside the covers!
Or your thumbs I'll paint hot mustard
To stop you spilling vital custard!

SPIKE:
Thank you, Matron, for those kind words,
The devil's in the detail.

MATRON:
The touching of your parts will prove a trial,
Until you learn the value of true self-denial.

SPIKE:
Thanks, Matron for the tip, but...
I have no energy for that trip.
Into the the realms of such erotica?
For me t'would prove a bridge too far.
Can we return to this scene's craft?
See! I have just shot my overdraft!
It had escaped from a London bank
And I'm being Percy if not Frank.

MATRON:
Oh for Ireland you have struck a blow!
You are a man I'm proud to know!

SPIKE:
This was an English overdraft.

MATRON:
I can see that. I'm not daft.
We shall make a proud elect
And go seek out the National Debt!

SPIKE:
Let's lay that demon on the altar,
From this resolve we shall not falter.
The National Debt we'll seek and slaughter
And free Great Britain ever after!
Let's spin again to make a trance!
Music! My fiddlers! Bring the dance!

Fiddlers enter playing a jig. SPIKE and the MATRON dance off accompanied by the capering musicians. They disappear into the distance...
DOCTOR:
Thus ends this tale with nonsense won
Our funding for this film is done.

* * * * *

I wrote The Lost Property Office, a sketch for *A Show Called Fred*. There is a recording of it featuring Peter Sellers in the BFI archives. I have no paper copy of it, so this is my memory of it. You may check it, should you care to, at your leisure, when you are next on London's South Bank.

"LOST PROPERTY OFFICE" sketch

CU sign, LOST PROPERTY OFFICE. CUT TO interior,

A lost property office. There are racks, but they contain not objects, but lost people – with labels attached. Their heads stick out at the end of the rows. Enter Peter Sellers, as character, MATE, a down-at-heel workman. He has a label tied round his neck. He is accompanied by an ATTENDANT who points out an empty rack. MATE climbs in, taking his place. The ATTENDANT exits. MATE recognises someone.

PETER / MATE:
Hello, mate!
FRIEND:
Hello mate! What are you doing here, mate?
PETER:
I got separated from my tools, mate, on the Circle Line, going to work today.

FRIEND:
You mean you lost your tools?
PETER:
No, mate, me tools lost me, didn't they? I'm lost mate. My tools, mate, they're wherever they are. They're probably going round the Circle Line, like I said. Where they was put, mate. How can they be lost? Mate?
FRIEND:
Until someone hands 'em in.
PETER:
No, mate, it was me that was handed in. Mate. It was me that was handed in! Cos I got separated, mate. From me tools!
FRIEND:
Well, the tools can't come and look for you, can they?
PETER:
I suppose they can't. No, mate. What happened to you?
FRIEND:
Well I got lost, mate, when my Missus threw me out.
PETER:
Who's going to claim you?
FRIEND:
Her sister might.
VALENTINE DYALL:
Keep quiet, damn you ! There are people trying to sleep in here!
PETER:
What happened to him?
FRIEND:
He got separated from his umbrella, mate, so he got handed in. He's had so many umbrellas, that man, and they're always losing him.
PETER:
Ain't it his umbrella wot was lost, mate?
FRIEND:
No, mate, now you got that wrong. That is not the new thinking, is it? How can an umbrella be lost? An umbrella is an object, mate. it is where it is.
PETER:
In the Universe?
FRIEND:
Right, mate.
PETER:
That's right, mate. Like my tools on the Circle Line. That's what I was

saying. They are where they are, mate. It's me that needs to be rejoined to them. Not them to me, mate. They don't care! How can a bag of tools care? How can tools feel lost without me? Eh, mate? It's me that feels lost without them.
FRIEND:
That's right, mate.

ATTENDANT *comes in with a gentleman's rolled umbrella.*

ATTENDANT:
Anyone recognise this umbrella?
VAL DYALL:
It's mine! I mean, we belong together, yes. Over here!
(Climbing off the rack)
Thank God, it's a miracle.
PETER:
How do you know that's your umbrella, mate? They all look alike?
VAL DYALL:
Well I don't look alike. I am properly labelled, so why don't you mind your own damn business?
ATTENDANT:
(Giving VAL DYALL the umbrella)
Congratulations.
VAL DYALL:
Joy! Joy!

ATTENDANT *and* VAL DYALL *exit.*

FRIEND:
Just makes it worse for the rest of us, don't it, mate? That joyful reunion?
PETER:
It gives me hope.
FRIEND:
Forget hope, mate. If you're not reclaimed within forty-eight hours, mate, forget it. Your bag of tools will have gone off with someone else.
PETER:
Oh, mate! I love my tools.
FRIEND:
Have you got a photograph of 'em?

PETER:
Yes, I have, mate...
(He produces old photo)
That's me and me bag of tools, mate. First day of work, building a h'arcade in Shepherds Bush, that fell down when a h'underground train shook it. They should've stopped the trains, mate. Then it wouldn't have fallen down...

Enter ATTENDANT with a scarf

ATTENDANT:
One wooly scarf! One wooly red scarf that has lost its person?
PETER:
No, mate, the person ain't been handed in yet, has he?
FRIEND:
No, he ain't.

ATTENDANT exits. With scarf.

PETER:
That was exciting, mate.
FRIEND:
Yes, mate. It goes on all day...

ATTENDANT enters with bag of tools.

ATTENDANT:
One bag of tools! Lost its owner on the Circle Line? Any offers?
PETER:
(Climbing off rack)
That's me, mate. I'm orf! Bye-bye. I hopes you gets claimed eventually mate. I think you'd have better luck with a wooly scarf than with a wife, mate. Why don't you change your label?
FRIEND:
I could get relabelled, mate. Thanks for the tip. Bye- bye!
PETER:
(Takes the bag of tools)
Bye-bye, mate...

PETER exits, carrying his tools. The ATTENDANT follows.

* * * * *

THE BAKER STREET RESIDENCE OF SHERLOCK HOLMES.

HOLMES is smoking his meerschaum pipe. WATSON hovers punching cushions. He goes to window where the curtains are drawn across and peers out.

WATSON:
Holmes, I have an apprehension that we were followed to our residence. We cannot so easily pick up a case and drop it at our leisure

HOLMES:
Though we are in residence, my dear Watson, the mind travels onward to new worlds where others cannot follow.

WATSON:
I do not have a passport to new worlds, Holmes, as I do not smoke opium.

HOLMES:
That is as may be. But listen to me. Our friend Mr Milligan – who can only find breath in absurdity – has recently committed himself to a mental hospital.

WATSON:
How do you know this?

HOLMES:
It is in the book, Watson. Where else would it be? While there Milligan assassinated his overdraft and dizzy with the feeling of freedom this act has given him he has left the clinic on a high note.

WATSON:
This is manic-depression. The highs are as dangerous as the lows. Stability – a middle ground – is the safest course.

HOLMES:
To where? The safest course is the most dangerous for it is one of utter delusion. Enough. The point is that Scotland Yard have been in touch with me.

WATSON:
About the exploding telephone box?

HOLMES:
No. About the National Debt. He intends – this Milligan fellow who I am minded to admire – to next assassinate the National Debt.

WATSON:
But Great Britain relies on it.

HOLMES:
That's why it is sinking us. You are too simplistic, Watson. But Milligan with his charms will entice the National Debt to leave the Treasury for an afternoon in the country.

WATSON:
The National Debt is a woman?

HOLMES:
It so happens, Watson. If it is a signal of being spendthrift then a man would do as well. However it is a woman, so be this Debt. And most seductive! She can outplay this Spike fellow at his own game.

WATSON:
That is possible, Holmes. Possibly not. It is all surmise. Which is why Scotland Yard wants us to protect her?

HOLMES:
No, rather we are to enable the crime.

WATSON:
Impossible! It is a treason, Holmes! We cannot be party to such a despatch of the National Debt!

HOLMES:
You do not understand economics. This mad Irishman must succeed. The country is bankrupt. Winning the war has ruined us.

WATSON:
Which war is that?

HOLMES:
Any war. The most recent one. The only hope – this from the highest levels – is that the National Debt be dissolved.

WATSON:
Dissolved?

HOLMES:
Yes. The body dissolved in a vat of sulphuric acid. Vat spelled V – A – T. Also known as Value Added Tax.

WATSON:
I really don't follow.

HOLMES:
We must go. Come, Watson. There is no time to lose.

WATSON:
I have a respectable overdraft limit and I keep within it. I love my overdraft and as far as the country is concerned I love the National Debt! Oh I don't know! I really don't....

They take their outdoor clothes and leave the apartment.

THE COUNTRYSIDE. A PLEASANT AFTERNOON.

On a blanket with a picnic hamper open are SPIKE and a beautiful woman. She lays back enjoying a glass of champagne while he plays the trumpet. Nearby, behind a tree keeping watch are HOLMES and WATSON.

HOLMES:
That's her.

WATSON:
Who?

HOLMES:
The National Debt, who else?

WATSON:
My God, Holmes. She is beautiful! Ravishing!

HOLMES:
She has Milligan in thrall. Fear not, he will not harm her.

SPIKE finishes his trumpet solo. She claps. SPIKE stands up. He produces an old fashioned duelling pistol and points it at her. She laughs and bares her bosom daring him to shoot her. He hesitates then fires the pistol into a tree disturbing the crows. She winds up an old fashioned gramophone and plays a scratchy dance tune. She arises and they dance off into the field.

CUT TO A BIG HERD OF CATTLE. THEY STAMPEDE. (Or stampeding buffalo / or elephants / or all three!)

SPIKE and the NATIONAL DEBT LADY hear the stampede. They run off. SPIKE makes it to a tree and climbs it. She trips before reaching safety and is lost in the stampede.

THE FLAT, BAKER STREET.

WATSON:
It was a terrible sight, Holmes! The National Debt was quite obliterated under the thundering of a thousand hooves.

HOLMES:
It has happened before. It will doubtless happen again. Quite elementary, my dear Watson.

WATSON:
It was hardly elementary. It was a stampede!

HOLMES:
Yes, it's called Galloping Inflation, Watson.

WATSON:
Galloping Inflation? What on Earth is that?

HOLMES:
That's what did for the National Debt. However beautiful and seductive she

is. Or was. Some things are inevitable. Fated to happen sooner or later. Now we can forget that subject. Where is my pipe?

WATSON:
Galloping Inflation? I see. Yes, yes, well maybe I don't see. There is a lot of Galloping Inflation about in the countryside, that's for sure. Beware the bull! And in some cities in Spain they encourage a day of the bulls, I would not take the National Debt there on holiday, however beautiful she was...

HOLMES:
Have you seen my pipe, Watson?

WATSON:
Don't go back to the opium, Holmes, I beg you. It will ruin you.

HOLMES:
Are we not already ruined?

WATSON:
No, no. Stand your ground sir, and suffer. You will find redemption in that.

HOLMES:
I do suffer, Watson. How much redemption can a man take? Have you hidden my pipe? Not again surely? It is a futile exercise. It is only my favourite pipe, I have a rack of other pipes.

HOLMES goes to the rack of pipes and selects one. He fills the bowl.

WATSON:
Where will it end, my dear Holmes? Where will it end?
HOLMES:
We do not know, Watson. We are only half way through the book...

HOLMES lights up contentedly.

* * * * *

"DEAD WAITER" sketch.

Spike Milligan, (BBC TV, Q5 or A Milligan For All Seasons)

A COUPLE are sitting in a restaurant. They have just finished their main course. The WAITER approaches with a tray to clear. He collapses over the table.

MAN:
Oh, dear…

He signals across the room. The MANAGER arrives.
MANAGER:
Oui Monsieur? Yes, sir, can I help you?
MAN:
It's about the waiter.
MANAGER:
You have a complaint about the waiter? The standard of service does not please you?
MAN:
No. As you can see, the waiter is ill…
MANAGER:
(Checks the waiter's pulse)
No sir, the waiter…he is not ill. He is dead.
WOMAN:
(Horrified)
Dead?
MANAGER:
Yes, madam, he has expired.
MAN:
I am glad we have established that…
MANAGER:
Will that be all, sir?
MAN:
All? What do you mean, all? You yourself has said this waiter is dead.
MANAGER:
Yes, but he was perfectly well when he left the kitchen. We do the best we can, sir, madam. You do not suggest that we give each of our staff a medical before they serve every table. Such is life…
MAN:
Hold on. We would like this waiter replaced.
MANAGER:
I see. Why?

MAN:
Because he is dead.
MANAGER:
You would like a fresh waiter?
MAN:
That's right.
MANAGER:
This one has not been rude to you?
MAN:
No, but he is not able to complete our order.
WOMAN:
We have not had our dessert yet.
MANAGER:
Ahh! I see!
MAN:
Exactly. As you can see, we have not been able to order the next course. Because the waiter – our waiter – is dead.
MANAGER:
Yes, I understand, sir. But the settlement of this waiter's affairs – including the unfinished business of ordering your dessert – and possible coffee – must now rest with his next of kin. A matter the management cannot afford to get involved in. It is a legal matter, sir, beyond our jurisdiction. So if you need to complete your order please get in touch with them...
MAN:
The waiter's next of kin?
MANAGER:
Yes. Please. Will that be all, sir?
MAN:
Yes, I suppose so. Thank you...

FILM: Graveside. A burial is in progress. CU: WIDOW, dabbing tears with a handkerchief.

The COUPLE approach. The MAN is holding a menu. He gets the attention of the WIDOW. MAN points at the menu.

SUBTITLE: WE WOULD LIKE TWO PEACH MELBAS PLEASE

Return to restaurant scene.
The COUPLE are waiting at the table (no dead waiter). The WIDOW,

dressed as at graveside, with black veil, approaches the table carrying a tray, and serves two peach melbas.

WIDOW exits. The COUPLE smile at each other, and eat their dessert. MANAGER approaches.

MANAGER:
Is everything alright, sir?
MAN:
Perfect, thank you…

The MANAGER slumps over the table, dead. The MAN leans over and feels the MANAGER's pulse. MAN signals to the WOMAN. He wipes his lips with a napkin, throws it down on the table.

The COUPLE exit.

* * * * *

Spike suggested that we go to the Hotel Leofric in Coventry to get away from it all while we wrote a Goon Show, THE GREAT STATUE DEBATE. So off by train, First Class, we went to this new and already famous hotel, one of the first to be built after the Second World War opening in 1955, a symbol of Britain's recovery boasting amazing innovations like sockets for electric razors. Spike had previously stayed at the hotel when he played at the Coventry Theatre.

At the time the Milligan was into 'Satyagraha' which was a form of deliberate holding to truth in acts of civil disobedience, espoused by Mahatma Gandhi. I borrowed the book he was reading on this subject and we discussed it over dinner…

SPIKE:
John, Satyagraha works for the Campaign For Nuclear Disarmament of which I am a supporter.

JOHN:
Me too.

SPIKE:
Satyagraha works in every area of life. For instance that rump steak you are eating dripping with blood is an act of violence against the animal

kingdom. That is why I am a vegetarian. Could you go into an abattoir and kill the cow or bull or even the baby calf that gives you veal?

I was chewing on my steak while he spoke…

JOHN:
No, I don't think so…
SPIKE:
You are separated from the act of violence that brings you meat, John. By shops and restaurants. Did you know that cows cry?

I swallowed my last piece of red meat to this very day…

JOHN:
No, Spike. Well I am done…
(I pushed the plate away)
If I shoot you I might eat you because I would not like to waste all that meat but what has a cow ever done against me? Or what have you done for that matter, Spike? That would turn me into a cannibal? No, that's it! My job is not to make cows cry but to bring joy into their lives. Cow laughter! We must find the nearest cowshed and see if we can cheer them up!

SPIKE:
The cows don't need cheering up, John. But the people who won the war and are losing the peace – they do! The Nation need cheering up. They need waking up! Let's just write this Goon Show and take the money home.

JOHN:
Isn't money an act of violence, Spike? If we act from love do we need to be concerned about making a living?

SPIKE:
That's why I love you, John. You will go on and suffer for the ideas you play with today. It is a cruel world. We must not let the bastards win.

JOHN:
Is that Satyagraha?

SPIKE:
If you had played the Coventry Theatre and tried to make those sneering

morons laugh you wouldn't talk to me about Satyagraha! I took a chair and sat on the stage and stared at the audience as they tried to boo me off. But they didn't win. Some actually started laughing and clapping and then I took out my trumpet and played to them.

JOHN:
I'm sure Gandhi would have been proud of you, Spike.

SPIKE:
Gandhi once met King George the Fifth. The King said, Didn't you have time to get dressed this morning? Gandhi replied, You wear Plus Fours, I wear Minus Fours! So he did have a sense of humour. But I tell you, John, if Mahatma Gandhi had ever played Coventry he would have ditched Satyagraha!

THE GREAT STATUE DEBATE came easily. It was fun to write. We laughed a lot and so did the cows!

> Hey diddle diddle,
> The Cat and the Fiddle,
> The Cow jump'd over the Moon!
> The little Dog laughed to see such fun,
> And the fork ran away with the spoon!

* * * * *

I wrote the following sketch for Peter Sellers in *The Jo Stafford Show*, circa 1962, in which he co-starred with the American singer. Not having the paper version or recording I have reinvented it...

"READING THE WILL" sketch.

A library of a country house. French windows to garden are open.
A table round which the various people (like Agatha Christie characters) are seated to hear the will being read out by the lawyer (PETER SELLERS). A pretty MAID hovers in the background. PETER has the will document in front of him. He blows the dust off it and opens it.

PETER:
Very well, let us begin. We are gathered here, in the library, for the reading

of the will of the Earl Trouser Minge-de-Groine, those assembled being the sole surviving and interested relations, friends or employees of the aforementioned groping earl...
(he opens the will)...
renowned for his good works, especially while incarcerated in Brixton jail for...? It does not specify. However his huge properties, estates, art treasures and shares in diamond mines survive intact-to, to be distributed according to this one and only will...
(reads out)
I, Roger, Trouser Minge-de-Groine, leave all my estate and everything I possess – solely to one person – my favourite relative....
(consternation around the table)
That relative being ... Quiet please... That relative to whom all is given, and to none other, being named as... as... as... Where was I?
(adjusts his glasses)
Ah, here we are... my nephew, Nigel FairPlay De-Groin
NIGEL:
(reacts in triumph)
Yes...!

A moment later he slumps across the table, dead. Consternation.

ANGELA:
He's been bitten by an Amazonian mamba. I'm afraid such a snake bite is fatal.
PETER:
Instantly?
ANGELA:
Oh yes...

The people are looking under the table for a snake.

BILL:
No sign of a snake.
LADY WINDERMERE:
I hate snakes!
VICAR:
It's gone to the garden! We are well rid of it!
PETER:
In that case I have no alternative but to proceed with the First Protocol. If

you will all resume your places, ladies and gentlemen, please…

Everyone calms down. PETER studies the document, and reads out…

PETER:
In the case of the decease of my nephew, Nigel Playfair, the residue of all my estates and fortune shall pass solely … solely, to my dear friend – and cellmate in the isolation wing at Brixton for certain perversions, The Reverend Hugh Jampton.

VICAR:
Praise the Lord !

Others gather round to congratulate the VICAR with such comments as, 'Couldn't have happened to a nicer person!' 'Congratulations!' Midst all this the VICAR slumps over the table. BILL examines him.

BILL:
It's a knife wound. Expert job. Between the ribs straight through the heart.

People look about them, anxiously.

PETER:
Is it another fatality?
BILL:
I'm afraid it is. Yes. The Reverend's a goner. Gone to glory. I would put it down as a suicide actually, because he couldn't bear the joy.
PETER:
I see. In that case we move on to Protocol Two. Ladies and gentlemen, if you would all please be reseated, thank you…
(Reads out)
In the event of the demise of the Reverend Hugh Jampton, I leave all my worldly goods to the best lay I enjoyed outside of my marriage, Lady Windermere.
LADY WINDERMERE:
I wouldn't have put it quite that way. Roger was a widower, you know, but… I'm sure the money will…

A shot rings out. LADY WINDERMERE slumps across the table. Anxiety.

PETER:
Dead?
BILL:
Yes, it could be a hunter, you know. A stray shot from the woods.
PETER:
In Surrey?
BILL:
Why not?
PETER:
If you say so. Press on then. Protocol Three! In the event of Lady Windermere's decease, I ... being the aforesaid Earl Trouser Press, De-Groine – whatever his name is... I leave all my worldly possessions reluctantly but entirely to my strange son Gaylord-Feathers-Minge-De-Groin.
GAYLORD:
(Dressed extravagantly, feather boa)
Oh my Gawd! The old man's coughed up at last, darling!

There is a sizzling noise. Smoke rises around GAYLORD. BILL gets to him.

BILL:
Unfortunate. Table lamp cord wrapped round his ankle. Electrocuted.
PETER:
In that case we have no alternative but to continue...
(Reads out)
Protocol Four. In the event of my son, Gaylord's decease I leave everything I own to my faithful and long suffering secretary, Angela Bins.
ANGELA:
Good, good! Rather than this ravenous set of vultures, at last my worth is recognised...

The survivors gather round. 'No ill will!' 'You deserve it if anyone does'.
BILL gives her a big hug! She slumps across the table. BILL checks her.

BILL:
Hard to credit. A broken neck.
PETER:
Resume your places.
BILL:
There's only me left...

(He sits down)
PETER:
I know. I am aware… Protocol Five. I, being of sound mind – I don't know why he didn't mention that before – the Earl Minge-de-Groine, leave all my worldly estates and possessions to my cheerful companion at the roulette tables and on African Safari Big Game Shoots of the Black Rhino, to… Bill Wyoming.
BILL:
Well there's a turn up, folks. Last in line, eh? You never know when your number's coming up.

BILL falls across the table. The MAID, who has been hovering in the background, runs forward to examine the body.

MAID:
He's drowned, sir.
PETER:
Drowned?
MAID:
Yes, he's soaking wet.
PETER:
You wouldn't expect that this far inland.
MAID:
No, sir. Well, well…
PETER:
He fell down the well? Possibly we did not notice. Sit down, my dear, this may be of interest to you…
MAID:
Yes, sir. Very well, sir…
(She sits at the table, avoiding the various bodies lying over it)
PETER:
Protocol Six. I, being whoever I am, the Earl De-Groine Trousers In The Cleaners… Leave all my worldly wealth to… to…
MAID:
Yes?
PETER:
To my solicitor! Joy my dear! We leave for the Caribbean this afternoon. Don't forget to pack your lingerie that I've been sending you under plain wrappers! Naughty me…!

PETER takes a drink. Falls across the table.

MAID:
(Checks his pulse)
The poor gentleman has had a fatal heart attack. Too much excitement. And what I slipped into his drink could help...
(She looks at the will)
That leaves Protocol Seven. To the maid! All written down it is! It was me who gave birth to the bastard Gaylord. His carry-on with the Downstairs staff? Wot? Well what goes round comes round! Better hand in me notice, hadn't I? I don't know who's going to clear up this mess. I'm off to the Riviera! Get a nice tan and a toy boy...!

The MAID exits with the copy of the will.

* * * * *

I was sitting beside Peter Sellers as he gunned his E-type Jag through the fog filling the Shepherds Bush road, a day in the fifties, that would be when I was new at the writing game a day when you could have smoked the smog. A car drifted past us coming the other way horn blaring our wing mirrors pinging. That was close...

Could you slow down, please, Peter? In these conditions I'd rather be out front waving a red flag. Peter laughed and slapped my knee. He liked to live dangerously. Fear not he said I have a guardian angel I cannot be harmed. Something else you should know Johnny I've spoken to Dan Leno at a seance recently which would interest you I'm coming to why. This should be Shepherds Bush look out for the Green.

I think we're driving across it...

Dan Leno told me through my medium – you've met Derek haven't you? He said – Dan Leno said that is – to whom I feel strongly linked in a previous life – Dan said no you weren't me in one of your previous reincarnations that's for sure you were my assistant think of that! He said – Dan Leno – you were so ambitious I had to let you go although I loved you for your talent for your passion you wanted everything I had he said including my mistress! You were like the twelve disciples he said, too much of a good thing. You were meant to betray me, all of you! I was like twelve disciples betraying Jesus I said? I'm Jewish! So were they...

The car mounted the pavement momentarily and bumped back down onto the road narrowly missing a Royal Mail red letter box reminding me I had a letter to post. Out of the fog loomed up the gates of the BBC TV Centre. We were met by Charlie with a limp, BBC Security, ex-Burma the Forgotten Army. Now he was forgotten by the BBC on the edge of their Empire at the barrier which he raised saluting smartly. Right-ho, Mr Sellers! Peter Sellers good for a Christmas box every year not like some of the mean bastards who come in looking like they own the joint...

Peter gunned the Jag through and braked into a skidding halt in from what we could see was a near empty car park. He jumped out. Come on, Johnny. Let's see who's in today. Ex-army officers most of 'em! Bomb happy the lot of 'em! Poor Charlie Security lost a leg in Rangoon. Most of these Light Ent producers lost their minds which was no big loss for the minor public school yobs who needed a war to get on a bit! Come on let's see if Tom's in – Head Of Comedy – Queens Regulations bloke but better than most – get your hair cut! That's the worst he'll say...

I followed Peter into reception. Deserted. Except for one soul behind the desk. What a surprise! Peter! She said. Someone brave enough to come in today. Hello Maisy! Peter blew a kiss. We were given identity tags and proceeded to the lift. Ping! It arrived and we were in and going up to the Fourth Floor. Peter was talking, I suppose because there was no-one else in the lift, big enough for a dozen people eager for fame...

So what happened? I asked Dan Leno, said Sellers. Through my medium Derek you've met Derek haven't you? I'll get him to do you one day. Dan Leno said I don't know what happened to you Peter I lost track of you I was at Drury Lane in pantomime and you went into the music hall circuit. I had my own troubles he said, the demon drink stay away from it. We were on the fourth floor walking round one of the endless circular corridors and bumped into Gilbert Harding – the celebrity brain-wave on the panel show What's My Line – he was coming the other way.

Hello Peter he cried out. Thank God for another human being!

Hello Gilbert I didn't recognise you with your clothes on. I am not a human being I am being human.

That's a significant difference said Gilbert. Do come to dinner Peter and bring that fascinating youth with you is he a model?

No he's a writer...

What a waste of a natural talent! Never mind. Next Thursday but you won't be free will you? You never are never mind I'll keep trying! Bring that hugely talented young whatever he is with you don't forget now! Gilbert Harding vanished up the corridor...

Peter picked up where he left off. So I went off with his bird Dan Leno's wife maybe or mistress he loved the two of us did Dan and he lost both of us in one go! Johnny that's a story of love and betrayal you write it up and I'll play Dan Leno right? You could play the assistant. Round the deserted corridor we went. We may have missed the Head of Comedy's office but we saw Gilbert coming towards us again because it was one circular hell and you could go round and round for ever. Gilbert cried out, Thank God because there is a God I do not intellectualise Him into the shadows which is the popular mode of the day. For Heaven's sake do send the tea trolley to me if you find it. I'm lost I die without succour. Refreshment! Human company being human! A map? A camel? What? Peter? Where are we? Let us dream up a show for TV together! We can if we think we can!

Any time, mate! I'll inform the Embassy Gilbert that you are up country and wish to return to Blighty where all will be forgiven. Gilbert was hanging on. Thanks! Do come to dinner! And bring the boy! Already I have plans for him great plans. I will help him open his first hair dressing salon! He's not a hairdresser Gilbert he's a writer. Never mind it does not mean he cannot improve himself. Harding's voice faded behind us as we pushed on...

The third time round the circular corridor was it the third – let's say so for luck – Sellers picked up the scent and pushed a door open. He burst into the offices of the Head of Light Entertainment. I trailed behind. Hello Maggie!

Peter!

Is he in, darling?

To you I'm sure he will be. Hang on, I'll phone through and let Tom know you are here. But Sellers was having none of it he was already at the inner sanctum door which he rapped upon as he opened it calling out, Hello Tom Lad! Avast you landlubber! Are you too busy picking your nose to see an unemployed actor?

Captain Tom who had commanded a company in the battle for Mount Casino and seen good men go down before the Poles stormed the heights and took the monastery responded yes I am here going through files rooting out Communists from Light Entertainment for that's what you expect me to be doing. Goodness, is that the Peter Sellers? Star of stage screen and Highgate Labour Exchange? Do come in! Or as you are already in – Get out! But abide awhile Peter, said Tom. There is always a welcome for you by my wastepaper basket. What brings you to the Beeb today?

I have an idea.

Then I will commission it immediately. Have you anything on paper?

That will come shortly from John Antrobus. Have you met him?

Yes, hello John. Get you hair cut, said Tom. I hope you're writing all this down, Antrobus? This memorable exchange.

He has an elephant's memory, said Peter.

It's more like an elephant's graveyard, I said.

As long as he is not a member of the Workers Revolutionary Party? There are already too many Reds in the Beeb whose aim is to overthrow the Government rather than to entertain. It does not make my job any easier.

Is there a black list on writers at the Beeb? I enquired.

Certainly not, John. What gave you that idea? This is a free country and the BBC must defend itself against any subversive influences. There is no black list but it operates. He smiled. Agreed some of my producer chaps are a bit O T T having difficulty realising they're back in civvy street wearing bowler hats instead of steel helmets. Do sit down everyone. Peter was already flopped into a chair. There's been no-one in today said Tom except my spies tell me Gilbert Harding is roaming the corridors looking for work. How did you manage to get through the fog?

Vith our latest miracle weapon, radar! explained Sellers. Vich I vill sell it to the BBC in exchange for passage to Brazil with Sophie Loren where I will reproduce a hundred Hitlers with my sperm and we get to keep the hotel towels! Zis would enable your employees Captain Tom to get to work through the most dense frog.

Frog? Don't you mean fog?

Silence ven you talk to me! I know vot I mean said Sellers. Froggy days are bad for productivity. Right, mate, that's enough of that he said in cockney. And that's enough of that too. Peter resumed what might be described as a normal voice. There is a tea dance at the Locarno, Streatham, this afternoon if you are not too busy, Tom?

Sorry. Too busy to go dancing. But do pitch this idea Peter, suggested the Head of Light Ent. I'm all ears.

Yes they are sticking out, said Peter. Would you be interested in John writing up a story where I play Dan Leno?

Tom replied promptly, Definitely. All leave is cancelled Antrobus until I get an outline which I will immediately commission. So stand up straight hands down the the seam of your trousers and don't forget that hair cut! You're working for the BBC now, laddie!

I told you he would say that said Peter as we walked in the corridor on the way back to the lift. We came across Gilbert Harding lying on a stretcher.

Are you alright, Gilbert? asked Peter.

I'm afraid the news is not good, Peter. I'm going to live.

I shouldn't worry about it, said Sellers. It won't last.

You are very well loved by the Public, Mr Harding, I added.

I can't get them all in my bed, said Gilbert. Could you possibly wheel me to the lift and deposit me in Reception where I may acquire an aspirin and a glass of water?

What happened to the people who helped you onto the stretcher, enquired Sellers.

They found me slumped against the wall completely isolated. On my own. Dying. Without a microphone. They gave me oxygen and then went home. Early today. Terrible weather. Getting worse. Can't see your hand in front of you by all report but I have no memory of it...

I wheeled Gilbert in the stretcher to the lift. While going down he said, Do come to dinner. I would like to help you with your career, Nigel. I'm sure I've got some good ideas.

John, I corrected him.

Do you have to be so particular he replied sharply. What's in a name? A rose by any other name would smell as sweet. And so do you. He continued to call me Nigel for the rest of his days. Which were numbered for Gilbert Harding would die on the steps of the BBC as it happened, but not on that day. That was the first and last I heard of the Dan Leno commission. It was an initiative that faded with a thousand other projects that Peter Sellers had wildly enthused over before disappearing to Hollywood leaving the wreckage of hopes other people had pinned on him. Fortunately I have a blessed inability to write to order on anything that does not capture my imagination so little was lost and that was a day...

* * * * *

The BBC commissioned me to write a play for a television series called *Comedy Playhouse*. AN APPLE A DAY was turned down flat as incoherent nonsense so I only got half a fee and of course no production. It was subsequently published under the book title, WHY BOURNEMOUTH, Calder & Boyars, and also received a successful stage production by the Ambience Theatre. Not that that would move anyone at the BBC TV Centre. Until...

I sent it to Peter Sellers who loved the play and told Michael Mills the latest Head of BBC TV Comedy that he would do it. Entranced by the prospect of securing the services of Peter Sellers now a Hollywood Super Star the BBC suddenly discovered merit in the absurd nature of the play and bought it all over again at an enhanced full fee! A date for production was set. Spike Milligan was cast in a cameo role. Plus the talented Kenneth Griffiths. All set to go…!

A week before rehearsal Peter Sellers disappeared. His agent, Dennis, carried the can without complaint. He was used to it. Hollywood had called and his client had flown away. It was too late to cancel the production without mayhem and cost and the producer was quickly able to recast Peter Cook and Dudley Moore who happened to be – and the being is everything! So it turned out very well after all and Peter Sellers had done me a favour rescuing the play. It was a nice production performed by beautiful comic talents!

"AN APPLE A DAY"

An extract :
Scene between MR ELMWOOD / Clive's father, (Peter Cook)
and MR THRUST, Muriel's father, (Spike Milligan).

ELMWOOD and THRUST sit by French windows sipping cocktails

ELMWOOD:
Arnold… I think it's about time we had a chat about the young couple… After all Clive and Muriel represent the future… They are tomorrow.
THRUST:
Tomorrow's Thursday, early closing…
ELMWOOD:
Precisely… Clive and Muriel are half day people… when we were young we had a much more definite attitude to life…
THRUST:
We hated it.
ELMWOOD:
Yes, it gave us something to live for… today young people are neither one thing nor the other… they're not even the third person… listen to this… I am… You are… He is… She is… you can't say that any more, can you… All you can say is 'I am You are He might be She certainly isn't and what the hell's going on here!' To be frank, Arnold, I'm extremely worried about Clive's genders… he doesn't seem to realise there are two of them…

THRUST:
Someone should tell him the facts of grammar...
ELMWOOD:
I've been too embarrassed... but somehow I must have a grandchild... someone to whom...
THRUST:
To whom... very good...
ELMWOOD:
To whom I can pass on...
THRUST:
The present tense!
ELMWOOD:
No, the wrestling arenas!

(Produced / broadcast BBC TV, 1972. Does anyone have a tape of this production?!)

* * * * *

WATERLOO STATION. DAY.

We pick up HOLMES and WATSON crossing the station concourse. HOLMES leads, carrying his violin case. WATSON follows, looking flustered.

WATSON. I say, Holmes, what is this all about? I have no idea! You are being very devious, sir, if I may say so...

HOLMES:
Here will do, my dear Watson. Waterloo Station. Under the clock.

WATSON:
Ah, that's it! Under the clock! Who are we meeting?

HOLMES:
No-one that I know of, Watson.

HOLMES removes violin from the case. Lays case open in front of him on the ground and tunes up the violin.

WATSON:
What are you doing? For Heaven's sake?

HOLMES:
I am establishing a presence, Watson.

WATSON:
A presence? By playing your violin in public? Can that be it? People will imagine that we are busking for money! You do realise that?

HOLMES:
People can imagine what they like. Mostly their imaginations are very limited. Meanwhile, my dear Watson, all donations should be gratefully received…

HOLMES starts playing the violin. Some people passing by drop money into the violin case. WATSON is flustered more than ever but responds politely.

WATSON:
No, you don't need to – we're not… Oh well thank you very much…
(to others)
No… well… Thank you… Thank you …We are not impecunious, madam – you don't need to… Thank you… oh well… thank you…thank you, no – so kind of you – no we don't have children waiting at home for a crust… Holmes! Holmes! Please! Desist! Desist! People think we do not have a pot to piss in!

HOLMES:
(Completes his violin piece and puts the violin aside)
You are a victim, my dear Doctor Watson. A slave to the good opinions of other people. It is a wretched condition. Let that be a lesson to you. Now count the money and tell me how well have we done?

HOLMES finds a bench and sits down. WATSON picks up the violin case and sits on the bench. He counts the money. A couple fashionably dressed and with smart luggage come and sit further along the bench.

PUBLIC ADDRESS:
Chimes
STATION MASTER:
The train for Cologne standing in Platform Five is now ready for boarding.

Passengers for the 13:15 train for Cologne please proceed to Platform Five.

MR SMITH:
That will be our train.

MRS SMITH:
Let me catch my breath. We've lots of time. Our seats are booked.

MR SMITH:
We have to stand up, pick up our luggage – my legs are a bit dodgy – and walk to the platform.

MRS SMITH:
Don't panic, Harry. The train won't leave without us, don't worry.

PUBLIC ADDRESS:
Chimes
STATION MASTER:
Will Mrs Smith please report to the Station Master's office.

MR SMITH:
Hello? That's funny. You're Mrs Smith.

MRS SMITH:
Yes, and you are Mr Smith. So what? How many Mr and Mrs Smiths do you think there are on Waterloo Station?

MR SMITH:
I suppose you're right...

PUBLIC ADDRES:
Chimes
STATION MASTER:
Will Mrs Hilda Smith who has booked on the train for Cologne please come immediately to the Station Master's office.

MR SMITH:
Hilda Smith you see? You're Hilda. And you're Smith. And you're going to Cologne?

MRS SMITH:
Exactly. So what are you waiting for? Come on…

PUBLIC ADDRESS:
Chimes
STATION MASTER:
Will Mrs Hilda Smith who is leaving for Cologne with that swine of a husband please come to the Station Master's office.

MR SMITH:
He's talking about me now!

MRS SMITH:
You don't need to get involved, Harry.

PUBLIC ADDRESS:
Chimes
STATION MASTER:
I love you Hilda. Since we met at the tea dance last October.

MR SMITH:
And I thought you were ice skating with Aunt Grechan? It's all coming out now, isn't it?

MRS SMITH:
Let's go to the train, Harry. Get up!

PUBLIC ADDRESS:
Chimes
STATION MASTER:
Do not go to Cologne, Hilda. Trying to start a new life there is taking your problems with you.

MR SMITH:
That's me. I'm the problem!

STATION MASTER:
Last call for Mrs Hilda Smith! Please come to the Station Master's office immediately. I cannot live a moment longer without you, darling!

MR SMITH:
You could do worse. He probably has a good pension too. Early retirement and free travel. If he was offering it to me...

MRS SMITH:
Don't be silly, Harry. It's a storm in a teacup...

PUBLIC ADDRESS:
Chimes. Then sound of a pistol shot. Pause.

WOMAN:
This is the last call for the 13:15 train to Cologne which will be shortly leaving from Platform Five.

The couple, MR and MRS SMITH gather up their luggage and leave.

WATSON:
What did you make of that, Holmes? A quite incredible scene.

HOLMES:
It was a sketch, my dear Watson.

WATSON:
A sketch?

HOLMES:
Yes, we are surrounded by sketches. We must be very careful. We cannot afford to become ensnared in that form of literature. The trouble is, Watson, and listen carefully, we – that is you and I – are out of copyright so any Johnny Come Lately can write us in to any scene or script or sketch that takes their fancy and what can we do about it? It seems little but perhaps by awareness we will be able not to cooperate. Now I see what Moriarty is after. Not the destruction of the Goons – that was a side show to lure us in – it is our destruction that Moriarty has long desired. By the pen of vacant minds! Come, come, Watson...

HOLMES has packed his violin in the case. He walks away.

WATSON follows...

WATSON:
I don't know what you're on, Holmes, truly? Well I do have some idea. If you could…? If you could – step by step – with me find your way back to some semblance of reality…

HOLMES: You call it reality Watson? Well you have your version of it. Come along, there's a good fellow. We have a concert to attend this evening…

* * * * *

A CONCERT HALL.

In the audience we find HOLMES and WATSON. Enter the ANNOUNCER

ANNOUNCER:
This evening we are fortunate to have with us in the studio two very well known musicians, Bradley and Jones! Yes, ladies and gentlemen, please welcome Two men, One piano!

BRADLEY and JONES, evening dress, enter. Take a bow and sit at a grand piano. JONES lifts the lid. BRADLEY poises above the keyboards – hushed silence – then starts playing a classical piece. JONES does not play and may occasionally acknowledge the audience with a smile… BRADLEY finishes with a flourish. They both get up and take a bow. The ANNOUNCER enters with a hand mike.

ANNOUNCER:
That was delightful. A truly wonderful rendering of the piece.

JONES:
Thank you. Thank you very much – it has been a great pleasure.

ANNOUNCER:
Yes…

JONES:
Oh yes…

BRADLEY:
(Says nothing. He just nods occasionally…)

ANNOUNCER:
Yes... I did notice – I hope you don't mind my mentioning it – that you were not actually playing.

JONES:
Yes. That is correct...

ANNOUNCER:
I thought I was...

JONES:
Yes. Yes, my partner, Giles Bradley. You see he does the playing.

ANNOUNCER:
Really? But I mean Two Men One Piano... If you don't mind my asking – why don't you both play?

JONES:
Well, there is no need, is there? It only takes one man to get a tune out of a piano..

ANNOUNCER:
I suppose that's true.

JONES:
Yes. Besides which I can't play a note anyway.

ANNOUNCER:
Really?

JONES:
Yes. Oh yes...

ANNOUNCER:
That is incredible...

JONES:
Yes, incredible. Mind you we all have our talents. Mine do not happen to lie in that direction. Nothing to be ashamed of there...

ANNOUNCER:
No, no, I wasn't suggesting... Tell me how did you come to team up with Mr Bradley?

JONES:
Well I used to be on my own you know.

ANNOUNCER:
As a pianist?

JONES:
Yes...

ANNOUNCER:
But I thought you said you didn't play the piano?

JONES:
That's right, yes. No, I mean that was the trouble. I wasn't getting the bookings. Good as I was at interviews!

ANNOUNCER:
Oh, quite. Quite...

JONES:
Hard times, yes. Yes... Finally I decided to team up with somebody who could actually play the piano and that's how I met Giles – Mr Bradley there – who was looking for a partner?

ANNOUNCER:
Why on earth would he do that?

JONES:
Well he's very shy onstage. Its very lonely out there under the spotlight. But now with the two of us he feels safer.

ANNOUNCER:
I must say I've never thought of it in that way, I could ask the other side of your partnership...

JONES:
No. Don't. Please. He would only panic. We each have our responsibilities – that's what makes any partnership – be it ever so humble. Yes…

ANNOUNCER:
Yes. Well… Thank you for that remarkable success story, Bradley and Jones!

JONES:
My pleasure. I've always been attached to pianos you know. I used to be a piano mover. That can involve a lot of heavy lifting…

ANNOUNCER:
(Speaks over Jones)
Thank you so much Two Men One Piano! Bradley and Jones! Ladies and gentlemen there will now be an interval commonly known as as the Jurassic Period. Thank you…

THE JUNGLE VEGETATION OF THE JURASSIC PERIOD.

Enter HOLMES and WATSON. They pause and listen. Sound of dinosaurs off. They peer through the undergrowth and see some dinosaurs rumbling through a clearing and disappearing back into the primeval jungle.

WATSON:
This is an uncommonly long interval, Holmes. It is worth asking in what part of the Jurassic Period we are cast? What on earth are we doing here?

HOLMES:
Everybody has to be somewhere, Watson. As Eccles of The Goon Show once so wisely remarked.

WATSON:
Does it not trouble you?

HOLMES:
It is not unusual, Doctor Watson, for a concert to have an interval.

WATSON:
Not one that lasts fifty six million years, Holmes – give or take fifteen

minutes. The last remark made more in hope than expectation.

HOLMES:
Watson, if you stand perfectly still – in the moment – there is no time, only a changing scene to which we are witness.

WATSON:
Yes, that is all very well, Holmes. But how the deuce do we get out of it?

HOLMES:
There is nothing to get out of. Except by an exercise of detachment.

There is a sound of something in the undergrowth. WATSON shows alarm.

WATSON:
There is something close by. It's all around us. Where is it? What is it? Did you bring your revolver?

HOLMES:
I do not usually bring a revolver to a concert.

A waiter appears with a tray of drinks.

WAITER:
Mr Holmes and Doctor Watson? Your interval drinks, gentlemen.

HOLMES and WATSON:
Thank you…

They take their drinks and the waiter disappears back into the undergrowth. They drink.

WATSON:
Oh well. Cheers….

They drink.

WATSON:
Two Men One Piano? That was a bit unusual…

HOLMES:
It was a sketch, my dear Watson. They are getting closer. Written by a trivial minded fellow who has fallen upon this means of making a living. Now he brings them together in a manner that unfortunately has come to involve ourselves. In this way he hopes to redeem his work. Never mind...

The interval bell rings. HOLMES rises.

HOLMES:
Let us return to the hall for the second half of this evening's performance.

WATSON:
How do you suggest we do that?

HOLMES:
By imaginative application, Watson. What brought us here can take us out by by the same means...

Sound of a helicopter. HOMES and WATSON make it to the edge of the clearing as the helicopter descends and lands. They run to it and are helped aboard. The helicopter takes off into the sky leaving behind the Jurassic scene as it heads out over the ocean.

* * * * *

Spike first played the *"TWO MEN, ONE PIANO"* sketch in *A Show Called Fred* and / or *A Milligan For All Seasons*.
Later Bernie took the sketch for the *Bernard Braden Show*.
The *"MEASUREMENTS"* sketch I wrote for Spike, he much liked it and played it more than once on his BBC television shows.

* * * * *

INT. BAKER STREET RESIDENCE.

HOLMES is smoking his pipe, relaxing. WATSON is knitting.

HOLMES:
What are you knitting, Watson?

WATSON:
The next scene, my dear Holmes.

HOLMES:
Well I hope you get the size right.

WATSON:
Of course.

HOLMES:
Where did you get the pattern?

WATSON:
From the book of course. The book of patterns. It helps me not to worry, Holmes. I fear we are helpless in this case – it is utterly beyond me to comprehend – so I took up this hobby of knitting scenes to take my mind off everything.

HOLMES:
It is a vain effort of control, Watson, but if it makes you feel better. However do be careful about answering the front door.

WATSON:
Why?

HOLMES:
There is a plague of sketches about, that's why. And your knitting more sketches is not helping. It is adding to the confusion. Do be careful. I recommend you do not answer the front door…

HOLMES leaves the room.

WATSON knits. Knock on door. Pause as WATSON hesitates. Another knock. Again WATSON continues with his knitting. A third insistent knock. WATSON throws down the knitting and goes to the door. He opens it to find SPIKE and JOHN in the hallway. They wear bowler hats.

SPIKE:
Good morning, sir or madam. We are from the Town Hall. We are here to check your measurements which will not take a moment…

SPIKE produces a tape and measures as he calls out to JOHN who jots down the details.

SPIKE:
Head eighteen.

JOHN:
Head eighteen.

SPIKE:
Chest forty-two.

JOHN:
Chest forty-two.

SPIKE:
Inside leg twenty-eight.

JOHN:
Inside leg twenty-eight.

SPIKE:
Thank you, sir or madam. We will be letting you know.

SPIKE and JOHN exit. WATSON closes the door and returns to the lounge – as HOLMES returns from an inner room.

WATSON:
They're going to let me know, Holmes.

HOLMES:
Who are?

WATSON:
The two chaps who took my measurements.

HOLMES:
What? What on Earth are you talking about, Watson?

WATSON:
Yes, they were just here. You missed them, yes. Pity. You could have given them yours.

HOLMES:
Given them my what?

WATSON:
Your measurements, Holmes. Yes. I think they were pretty pleased with my measurements. I must say, yes...

HOLMES:
Who were?

WATSON:
They said they were from the Town Hall.

HOLMES:
Did they show you any credentials?

WATSON:
I didn't think to ask.

HOLMES:
You answer the door and you let two strangers take your measurements, Watson? Am I hearing this right?

WATSON:
There's nothing wrong with my measurements, Holmes. What are you implying? A good head eighteen! Chest forty-two! And an inside leg of twenty-eight. I thought it was thirty but I'm happy to settle for twenty-nine... most days.

HOLMES:
That's not the point. You stand on the doorstep giving your measurements to anyone who knocks on the door.

WATSON:
I was trying to be helpful.

HOLMES:
Were you now?

WATSON:
Yes.

HOLMES:
Well they took Mr Jones' measurements last week and look what happened to him.

WATSON:
I don't know what happened to him.

HOLMES:
He disappeared, didn't he?

WATSON:
Did he?

HOLMES:
Yes, the day after they took his measurements.

WATSON:
That does not entirely surprise me, the poor shape Mr Jones was in. Frankly I could not see him passing.

HOLMES:
Passing what?

WATSON:
Well whatever it is one has to pass. I have no regrets. No fears whatsoever, Holmes...

WATSON happens to come by the window. He peers out. Steps back in alarm.

WATSON:
Oh my God!

HOLMES:
What is it, Watson?

WATSON:
(Peering out again from behind the curtains)
It's Mr Jones. They've changed his measurements...

HOLMES:
Calm down, Watson. We are in a sketch. Deeply entrenched. It has happened as I predicted. Through one act of your carelessness...

WATSON:
Does that make it any less real?

HOLMES:
No, we must see it through if life offers us nothing else.
(Filling his pipe)
Fear not, my dear Doctor. There are other authors – other books – where we shall breathe again – have adventures – and be treated with the respect my reputation deserves. What's done is done. Being out of copyright was always going to be a problem for us – sooner or later – and now it's happened. I do not expect you to comprehend dimensions that have not been revealed to you. I am firmly established in this dreadful author's mind. So much so that I can take control of him. This book shall be terminated. Brought to an abrupt end. These are the last pages. Behind all still lies Count Moriarty who has used this witless device to denigrate our characters. But he has failed in this endeavour. All in all we have not come out of it badly and – and other adventures beckon.

WATSON:
But... But... Surely...? Holmes...? If there is a shred of reality in your words – words that I have trusted in times past – though outrageous, none like this... Consider – please... This may not be the best life, my dear Holmes, but it is the only one we have, here and now.

HOLMES:
Yes. And so it concludes. As all episodes must. As life picks us up again and carries us into the Great Unknown...

HOLMES inhales on his pipe contentedly.

THE END

(Deep breath. The book ends but you are safe in your foreverness.)

www.ingramcontent.com/pod-product-compliance
Lightning Source LLC
Chambersburg PA
CBHW070935160426
43193CB00011B/1694